Microsoft Word 2000 Simplified™

IDG's 3-D Visual™ Series

IDG
BOOKS

From
maranGraphics™

IDG Books Worldwide, Inc.
An International Data Group Company
Foster City, CA • Indianapolis • Chicago • New York

Microsoft® Word 2000 Simplified™

Published by
IDG Books Worldwide, Inc.
An International Data Group Company
919 E. Hillsdale Blvd., Suite 400
Foster City, CA 94404
(650) 655-3000

Copyright© 1999 by maranGraphics Inc.
5755 Coopers Avenue
Mississauga, Ontario, Canada
L4Z 1R9

Library of Congress Catalog Card No.: 99-62446
ISBN: 0-7645-6054-9
Printed in the United States of America
10 9 8 7 6 5 4 3 2 1

Distributed in the United States by IDG Books Worldwide, Inc.
Distributed by CDG Books Canada Inc. for Canada; by Transworld Publishers Limited in the United Kingdom; by IDG Norge Books for Norway; by IDG Sweden Books for Sweden; by Woodslane Pty. Ltd. for Australia; by Woodslane (NZ) Ltd. for New Zealand; by TransQuest Publishers Pte Ltd. for Singapore, Malaysia, Thailand, Indonesia, and Hong Kong; by ICG Muse, Inc. for Japan; by Norma Comunicaciones S.A. for Colombia; by Intersoft for South Africa; by Le Monde en Tique for France; by International Thomson Publishing for Germany, Austria and Switzerland; by Distribuidora Cuspide for Argentina; by Livraria Cultura for Brazil; by Ediciones ZETA S.C.R. Ltda. for Peru; by WS Computer Publishing Corporation, Inc., for the Philippines; by Contemporanea de Ediciones for Venezuela; by Express Computer Distributors for the Caribbean and West Indies; by Micronesia Media Distributor, Inc. for Micronesia; by Grupo Editorial Norma S.A. for Guatemala; by Chips Computadoras S.A. de C.V. for Mexico; by Editorial Norma de Panama S.A. for Panama; by American Bookshops for Finland. Authorized Sales Agent: Anthony Rudkin Associates for the Middle East and North Africa.
For corporate orders, please call maranGraphics at 800-469-6616.
For general information on IDG Books Worldwide's books in the U.S., please call our Consumer Customer Service department at 800-762-2974.
For reseller information, including discounts and premium sales, please call our Reseller Customer Service department at 800-434-3422.
For information on where to purchase IDG Books Worldwide's books outside the U.S., please contact our International Sales department at 317-596-5530 or fax 317-596-5692.
For consumer information on foreign language translations, please contact our Customer Service department at 1-800-434-3422, fax 317-596-5692, or e-mail rights@idgbooks.com.
For information on licensing foreign or domestic rights, please phone 1-650-655-3109.
For sales inquiries and special prices for bulk quantities, please contact our Sales department at 650-655-3200.
For information on using IDG Books Worldwide's books in the classroom or for ordering examination copies, please contact our Educational Sales department at 800-434-2086 or fax 317-596-5499.
For press review copies, author interviews, or other publicity information, please contact our Public Relations department at 650-655-3000 or fax 650-655-3299.
For authorization to photocopy items for corporate, personal, or educational use, please contact maranGraphics at 800-469-6616.

Trademark Acknowledgments

Permission

ABOUT IDG BOOKS WORLDWIDE

Welcome to the world of IDG Books Worldwide.

IDG Books Worldwide, Inc., is a subsidiary of International Data Group, the world's largest publisher of computer-related information and the leading global provider of information services on information technology. IDG was founded more than 30 years ago by Patrick J. McGovern and now employs more than 9,000 people worldwide. IDG publishes more than 290 computer publications in over 75 countries. More than 90 million people read one or more IDG publications each month.

Launched in 1990, IDG Books Worldwide is today the #1 publisher of best-selling computer books in the United States. We are proud to have received eight awards from the Computer Press Association in recognition of editorial excellence and three from Computer Currents' First Annual Readers' Choice Awards. Our best-selling ...For Dummies® series has more than 50 million copies in print with translations in 31 languages. IDG Books Worldwide, through a joint venture with IDG's Hi-Tech Beijing, became the first U.S. publisher to publish a computer book in the People's Republic of China. In record time, IDG Books Worldwide has become the first choice for millions of readers around the world who want to learn how to better manage their businesses.

Our mission is simple: Every one of our books is designed to bring extra value and skill-building instructions to the reader. Our books are written by experts who understand and care about our readers. The knowledge base of our editorial staff comes from years of experience in publishing, education, and journalism — experience we use to produce books to carry us into the new millennium. In short, we care about books, so we attract the best people. We devote special attention to details such as audience, interior design, use of icons, and illustrations. And because we use an efficient process of authoring, editing, and desktop publishing our books electronically, we can spend more time ensuring superior content and less time on the technicalities of making books.

You can count on our commitment to deliver high-quality books at competitive prices on topics you want to read about. At IDG Books Worldwide, we continue in the IDG tradition of delivering quality for more than 30 years. You'll find no better book on a subject than one from IDG Books Worldwide.

John Kilcullen
Chairman and CEO
IDG Books Worldwide, Inc.

Steven Berkowitz
President and Publisher
IDG Books Worldwide, Inc.

IDG is the world's leading IT media, research and exposition company. Founded in 1964, IDG had 1997 revenues of $2.05 billion and has more than 9,000 employees worldwide. IDG offers the widest range of media options that reach IT buyers in 75 countries representing 95% of worldwide IT spending. IDG's diverse product and services portfolio spans six key areas including print publishing, online publishing, expositions and conferences, market research, education and training, and global marketing services. More than 90 million people read one or more of IDG's 290 magazines and newspapers, including IDG's leading global brands — Computerworld, PC World, Network World, Macworld and the Channel World family of publications. IDG Books Worldwide is one of the fastest-growing computer book publishers in the world, with more than 700 titles in 36 languages. The "...For Dummies®" series alone has more than 50 million copies in print. IDG offers online users the largest network of technology-specific Web sites around the world through IDG.net (http://www.idg.net), which comprises more than 225 targeted Web sites in 55 countries worldwide. International Data Corporation (IDC) is the world's largest provider of information technology data, analysis and consulting, with research centers in over 41 countries and more than 400 research analysts worldwide. IDG World Expo is a leading producer of more than 168 globally branded conferences and expositions in 35 countries including E3 (Electronic Entertainment Expo), Macworld Expo, ComNet, Windows World Expo, ICE (Internet Commerce Expo), Agenda, DEMO, and Spotlight. IDG's training subsidiary, ExecuTrain, is the world's largest computer training company, with more than 230 locations worldwide and 785 training courses. IDG Marketing Services helps industry-leading IT companies build international brand recognition by developing global integrated marketing programs via IDG's print, online and exposition products worldwide. Further information about the company can be found at www.idg.com.   1/24/99

maranGraphics is a family-run business located near Toronto, Canada.

At **maranGraphics**, we believe in producing great computer books–one book at a time.

Each maranGraphics book uses the award-winning communication process that we have been developing over the last 25 years. Using this process, we organize screen shots, text and illustrations in a way that makes it easy for you to learn new concepts and tasks.

We spend hours deciding the best way to perform each task, so you don't have to! Our clear, easy-to-follow screen shots and instructions walk you through each task from beginning to end.

Our detailed illustrations go hand-in-hand with the text to help reinforce the information. Each illustration is a labor of love–some take up to a week to draw!

We want to thank you for purchasing what we feel are the best computer books money can buy. We hope you enjoy using this book as much as we enjoyed creating it!

Sincerely,

The Maran Family

Please visit us on the web at:
www.maran.com

Credits

Author & Architect:
Ruth Maran

Copy Editors:
Cathy Benn
Jill Maran

Project Manager:
Judy Maran

Editing & Screen Captures:
Raquel Scott
Janice Boyer
Michelle Kirchner
James Menzies
Frances Lea
Emmet Mellow

Layout Designer:
Treena Lees

Illustrators:
Russ Marini
Jamie Bell
Peter Grecco
Sean Johannesen
Steven Schaerer

Screen Artist & Corrections:
Jimmy Tam

Indexer:
Raquel Scott

Post Production:
Robert Maran

Editorial Support:
Michael Roney

Acknowledgments

Thanks to the dedicated staff of maranGraphics, including
Jamie Bell, Cathy Benn, Janice Boyer, Francisco Ferreira,
Peter Grecco, Jenn Hillman, Sean Johannesen, Michelle Kirchner,
Wanda Lawrie, Frances Lea, Treena Lees, Jill Maran, Judy Maran,
Maxine Maran, Robert Maran, Sherry Maran, Russ Marini,
Emmet Mellow, James Menzies, Steven Schaerer, Raquel Scott,
Jimmy Tam, Roxanne Van Damme, Paul Whitehead
and Kelleigh Wing.

Finally, to Richard Maran who originated the easy-to-use
graphic format of this guide. Thank you for your
inspiration and guidance.

Table of Contents

CHAPTER 4

EDIT TEXT

CHAPTER 5

FORMAT TEXT

Table of Contents

CHAPTER 6

FORMAT PAGES

CHAPTER 7

PRINT DOCUMENTS

CHAPTER 8

WORK WITH MULTIPLE DOCUMENTS

CHAPTER 9

WORK WITH TABLES

CHAPTER 10

WORK WITH GRAPHICS

CHAPTER 11

MAIL MERGE

CHAPTER 12

WORD AND THE INTERNET

Mr. Adams:
I am delighted to inform you that your
company has been selected to receive
a Community Spirit Award.

Your staff's efforts to raise money to buy
new equipment for the local hospital are
admirable.

A reception will be held to honor you a
the other winners at Breton Banq
at 8 p.m. on July 12.

Nancy L. Spencer, Chairperson
Community Spirit Awards Committee

admirable

CHAPTER 1

GETTING STARTED

Are you ready to begin using Microsoft Word 2000? This chapter will help you get started.

100%

Word lets you efficiently produce professional-looking documents, such as letters, reports, essays and newsletters.

Edit Documents

Word offers many features that help you edit text in a document. You can add, delete and rearrange text. You can also check your document for spelling and grammar errors and use Word's built-in thesaurus to find more suitable words.

Format Documents

You can format a document to enhance the appearance of the document. You can use various fonts, styles and colors to emphasize important text. You can also center text on a page, adjust the spacing between lines of text, change the margins and create newspaper columns.

Print Documents

You can produce a paper copy of a document you create. Before printing, you can preview how the document will appear on a printed page. You can also print envelopes and mailing labels.

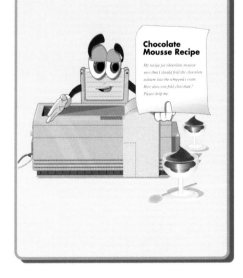

Create Tables

You can create tables to neatly display columns of information in a document. You can use one of Word's ready-to-use designs to instantly enhance the appearance of a table you create.

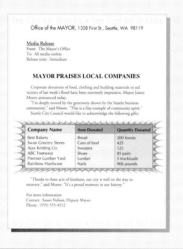

Add Graphics

Word comes with many types of graphics that you can use to make a document more interesting and entertaining. You can add graphics such as AutoShapes, text effects and clip art images.

Mail Merge

You can quickly produce personalized letters and mailing labels for each person on a mailing list. This is useful if you often send the same document, such as an announcement or advertisement, to many people.

Word and the Internet

You can save a document as a Web page. This lets you place the document on the Internet for other people to view. You can also add a hyperlink to a document to connect the document to a Web page.

A mouse is a handheld device that lets you select and move items on your screen.

When you move the mouse on your desk, the mouse pointer on your screen moves in the same direction. The mouse pointer assumes different shapes, such as ↕ or I, depending on its location on your screen and the task you are performing.

Resting your hand on the mouse, use your thumb and two rightmost fingers to move the mouse on your desk. Use your two remaining fingers to press the mouse buttons.

MOUSE ACTIONS

Click

Press and release the left mouse button.

Double-click

Quickly press and release the left mouse button twice.

Right-click

Press and release the right mouse button.

Drag

Position the mouse pointer (↕) over an object on your screen and then press and hold down the left mouse button. Still holding down the button, move the mouse to where you want to place the object and then release the button.

START WORD

When you start Word, a blank document appears on your screen. You can type text into this document.

START WORD

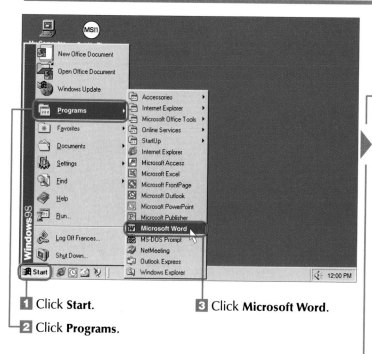

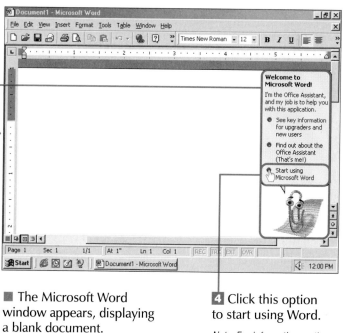

1 Click **Start**.

2 Click **Programs**.

3 Click **Microsoft Word**.

■ The Microsoft Word window appears, displaying a blank document.

■ The Office Assistant welcome appears the first time you start Word.

4 Click this option to start using Word.

Note: For information on the Office Assistant, see page 18.

7

THE WORD SCREEN

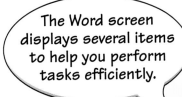

The Word screen displays several items to help you perform tasks efficiently.

Standard Toolbar

Contains buttons to help you select common commands, such as Save and Print.

Insertion Point

The flashing line on the screen that indicates where the text you type will appear.

Formatting Toolbar

Contains buttons to help you select common formatting commands, such as Bold and Underline.

Ruler

Allows you to change margin and tab settings for the document.

Status Bar

Provides information about the area of the document displayed on the screen and the position of the insertion point.

Page 1

The page displayed on the screen.

At 1"

The distance from the top of the page to the insertion point.

Sec 1

The section of the document displayed on the screen.

Ln 1

The number of lines from the top margin to the insertion point.

1/1

The page displayed on the screen and the total number of pages in the document.

Col 1

The number of characters from the left margin to the insertion point, including spaces.

SELECT COMMANDS USING TOOLBARS

> A toolbar contains buttons that you can use to select commands. Each command performs a different task.

TOOLBARS

When you first start Word, the most commonly used buttons appear on each toolbar. As you work with Word, the toolbars automatically change to remove buttons you rarely use and display the buttons you use most often.

SELECT COMMANDS USING TOOLBARS

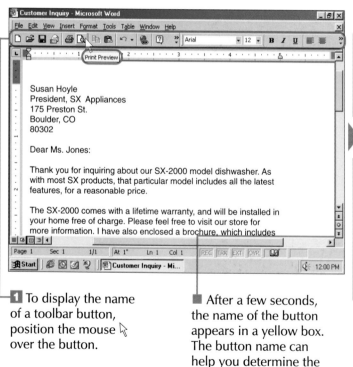

1 To display the name of a toolbar button, position the mouse ↖ over the button.

■ After a few seconds, the name of the button appears in a yellow box. The button name can help you determine the task the button performs.

2 A toolbar may not be able to display all of its buttons. Click ⁇ to display additional buttons for the toolbar.

■ Additional buttons for the toolbar appear.

3 To use a toolbar button to select a command, click the button.

You can select a command from a menu to perform a task. Each command performs a different task.

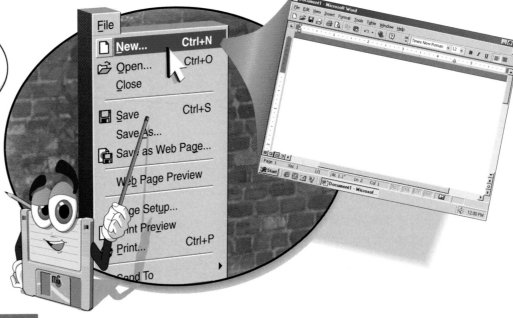

SELECT COMMANDS USING MENUS

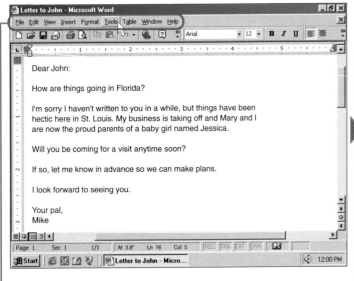

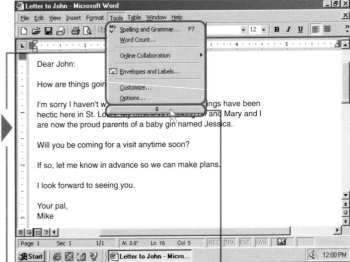

1 Click the name of the menu you want to display.

■ A short version of the menu appears, displaying the most commonly used commands.

2 To expand the menu and display all the commands, position the mouse ⩗ over ⩗.

Note: If you do not perform step 2, the expanded menu will automatically appear after a few seconds.

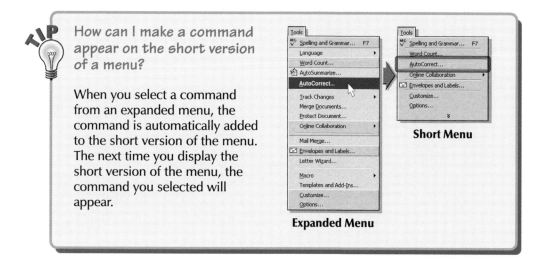

TIP

How can I make a command appear on the short version of a menu?

When you select a command from an expanded menu, the command is automatically added to the short version of the menu. The next time you display the short version of the menu, the command you selected will appear.

Short Menu

Expanded Menu

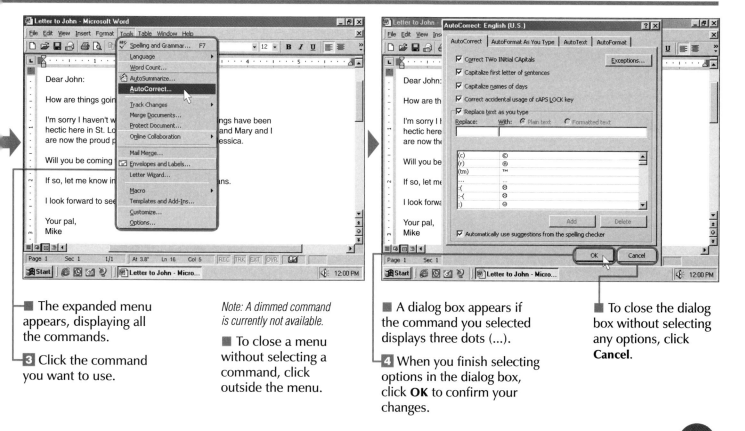

■ The expanded menu appears, displaying all the commands.

3 Click the command you want to use.

Note: A dimmed command is currently not available.

■ To close a menu without selecting a command, click outside the menu.

■ A dialog box appears if the command you selected displays three dots (...).

4 When you finish selecting options in the dialog box, click **OK** to confirm your changes.

■ To close the dialog box without selecting any options, click **Cancel**.

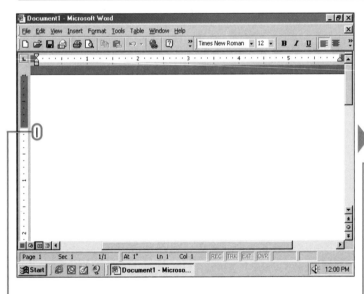

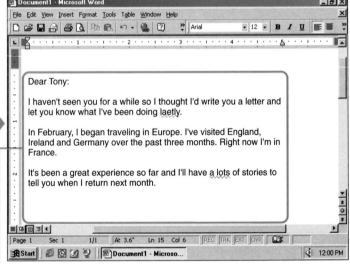

■ The text you type will appear where the insertion point flashes on your screen.

1 Type the text for your document.

■ When the text you type reaches the end of a line, Word automatically wraps the text to the next line. You only need to press the **Enter** key when you want to start a new paragraph.

Note: In this example, the font of text was changed to Arial to make the document easier to read. To change the font of text, see page 76.

12

TIP

Can I enter text anywhere in my document?

Word's Click and Type feature allows you to enter text anywhere in your document. Double-click the location where you want to enter text and then type the text. The Click and Type feature is only available in the Print Layout and Web Layout views. For more information on the views, see page 34.

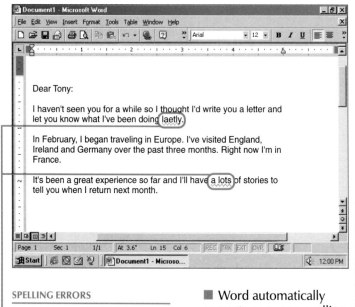

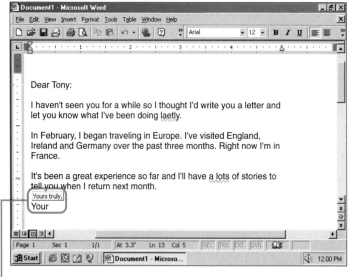

SPELLING ERRORS

■ Word automatically underlines spelling errors in red and grammar errors in green. The underlines will not appear when you print your document. To correct spelling and grammar errors, see pages 58 to 61.

■ Word automatically corrects common spelling errors as you type, such as recieve (receive) and nwe (new).

ENTER TEXT AUTOMATICALLY

■ Word's AutoText feature helps you quickly enter common words and phrases.

■ When you type the first few characters of a common word or phrase, a yellow box appears, displaying the text.

1 To insert the text, press the `Enter` key.

■ To ignore the text, continue typing.

Note: For more information on the AutoText feature, see pages 68 to 71.

Before performing many tasks in Word, you must select the text you want to work with. Selected text appears highlighted on your screen.

admirable

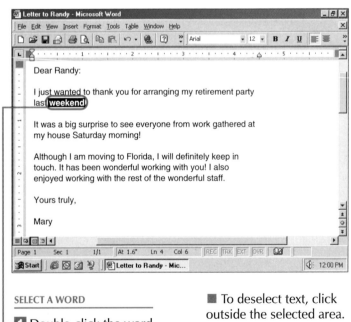

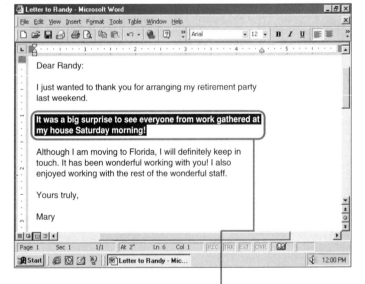

SELECT A WORD

1 Double-click the word you want to select.

■ To deselect text, click outside the selected area.

SELECT A SENTENCE

1 Press and hold down the Ctrl key.

2 Still holding down the Ctrl key, click the sentence you want to select.

TIP

How do I select all the text in my document?

To quickly select all the text in your document, press and hold down the `Ctrl` key as you press the `A` key.

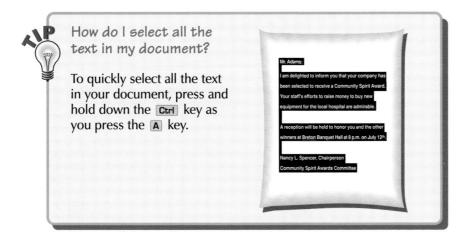

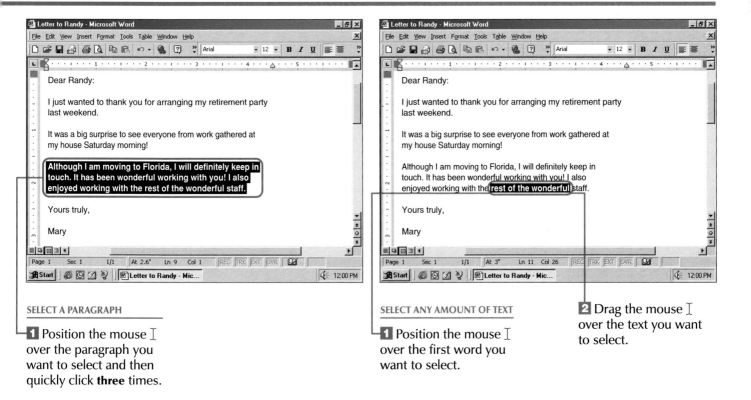

SELECT A PARAGRAPH

1 Position the mouse I over the paragraph you want to select and then quickly click **three** times.

SELECT ANY AMOUNT OF TEXT

1 Position the mouse I over the first word you want to select.

2 Drag the mouse I over the text you want to select.

MOVE THROUGH A DOCUMENT

You can easily move to another location in your document.

If you create a long document, your computer screen may not be able to display all the text at once. You must scroll through your document to view other parts of the document.

MOVE THROUGH A DOCUMENT

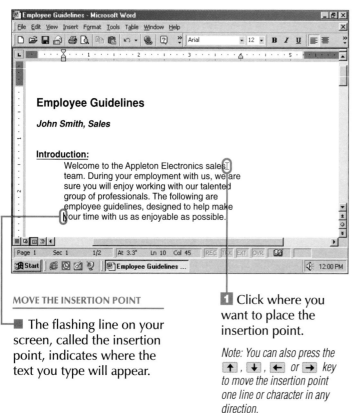

MOVE THE INSERTION POINT

■ The flashing line on your screen, called the insertion point, indicates where the text you type will appear.

1 Click where you want to place the insertion point.

Note: You can also press the ↑, ↓, ← or → key to move the insertion point one line or character in any direction.

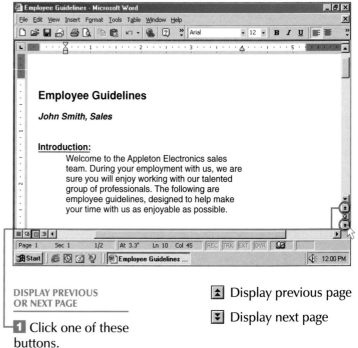

DISPLAY PREVIOUS OR NEXT PAGE

1 Click one of these buttons.

⬆ Display previous page

⬇ Display next page

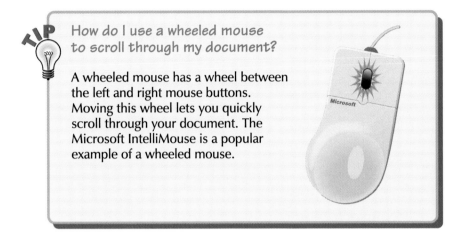

TIP

How do I use a wheeled mouse to scroll through my document?

A wheeled mouse has a wheel between the left and right mouse buttons. Moving this wheel lets you quickly scroll through your document. The Microsoft IntelliMouse is a popular example of a wheeled mouse.

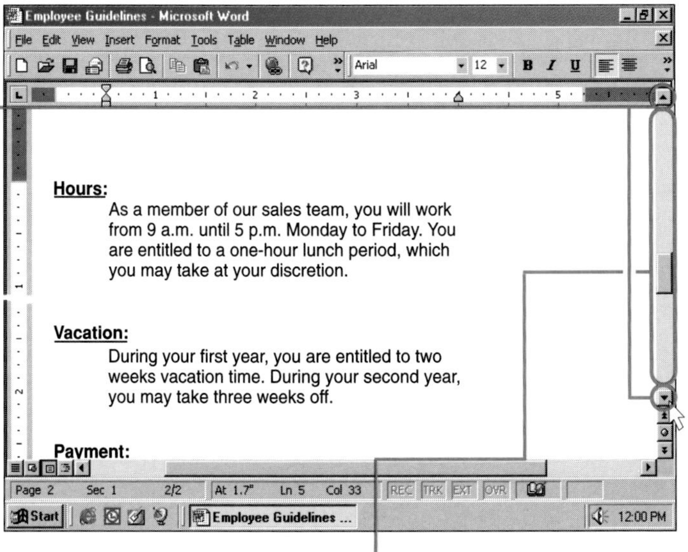

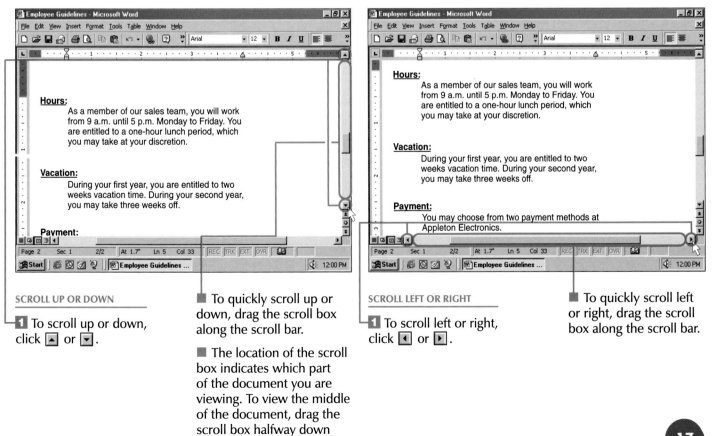

SCROLL UP OR DOWN

1 To scroll up or down, click ▲ or ▼.

■ To quickly scroll up or down, drag the scroll box along the scroll bar.

■ The location of the scroll box indicates which part of the document you are viewing. To view the middle of the document, drag the scroll box halfway down the scroll bar.

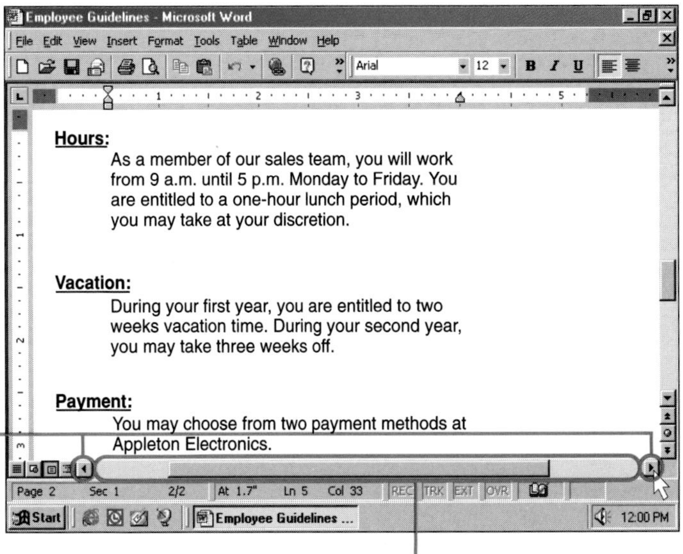

SCROLL LEFT OR RIGHT

1 To scroll left or right, click ◀ or ▶.

■ To quickly scroll left or right, drag the scroll box along the scroll bar.

GETTING HELP

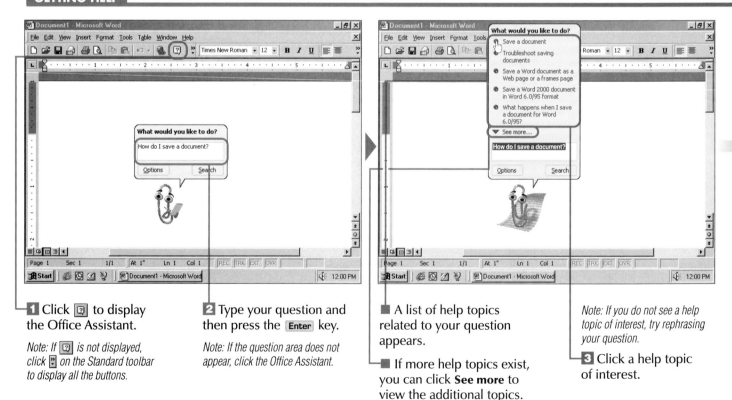

1 Click 🗐 to display the Office Assistant.

Note: If 🗐 is not displayed, click ⬚ on the Standard toolbar to display all the buttons.

2 Type your question and then press the **Enter** key.

Note: If the question area does not appear, click the Office Assistant.

■ A list of help topics related to your question appears.

■ If more help topics exist, you can click **See more** to view the additional topics.

Note: If you do not see a help topic of interest, try rephrasing your question.

3 Click a help topic of interest.

18

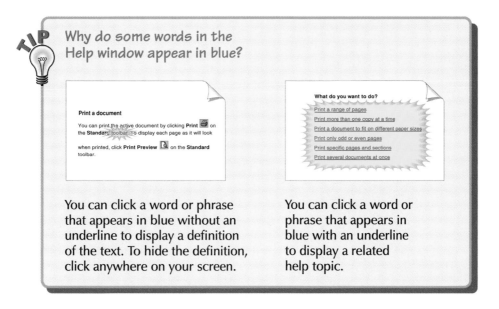

Why do some words in the Help window appear in blue?

You can click a word or phrase that appears in blue without an underline to display a definition of the text. To hide the definition, click anywhere on your screen.

You can click a word or phrase that appears in blue with an underline to display a related help topic.

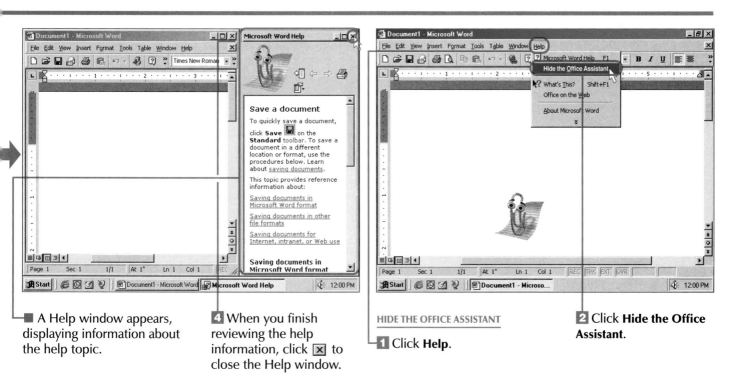

■ A Help window appears, displaying information about the help topic.

4 When you finish reviewing the help information, click ☒ to close the Help window.

HIDE THE OFFICE ASSISTANT

1 Click **Help**.

2 Click **Hide the Office Assistant**.

CHAPTER 2

SAVE AND OPEN DOCUMENTS

Are you wondering how to save, close or open a Word document? Learn how in this chapter.

SAVE A DOCUMENT

You can save your document to store it for future use. This allows you to later review and edit the document.

You should regularly save changes you make to a document to avoid losing your work.

SAVE A DOCUMENT

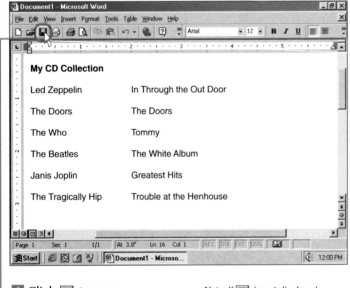

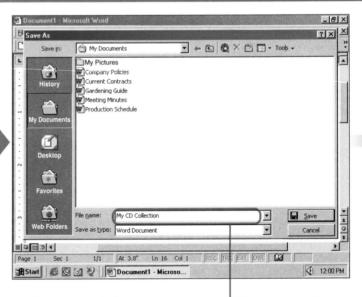

1 Click 🖫 to save your document.

Note: If 🖫 is not displayed, click 💱 on the Standard toolbar to display all the buttons.

■ The Save As dialog box appears.

Note: If you previously saved your document, the Save As dialog box will not appear since you have already named the document.

2 Type a name for the document.

TIP

What are the commonly used
folders I can access?

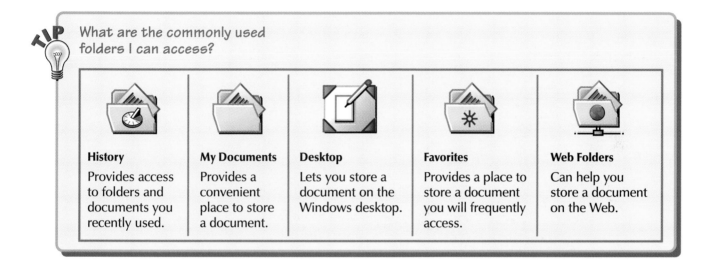

History

Provides access
to folders and
documents you
recently used.

My Documents

Provides a
convenient
place to store
a document.

Desktop

Lets you store a
document on the
Windows desktop.

Favorites

Provides a place to
store a document
you will frequently
access.

Web Folders

Can help you
store a document
on the Web.

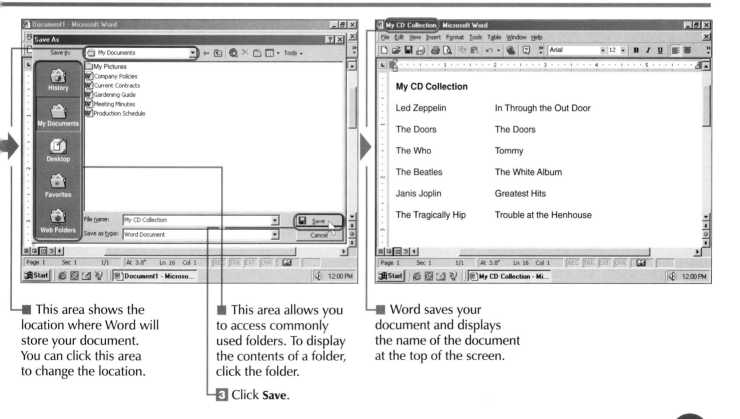

■ This area shows the
location where Word will
store your document.
You can click this area
to change the location.

■ This area allows you
to access commonly
used folders. To display
the contents of a folder,
click the folder.

3 Click **Save**.

■ Word saves your
document and displays
the name of the document
at the top of the screen.

When you finish working with a document, you can close the document to remove it from your screen.

When you close a document, you do not exit the Word program. You can continue to work with other documents.

CLOSE A DOCUMENT

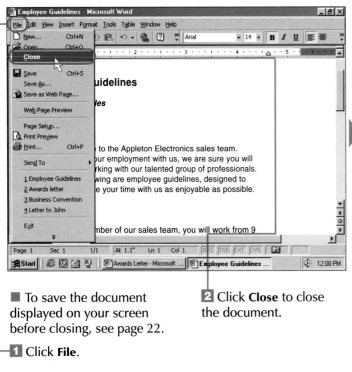

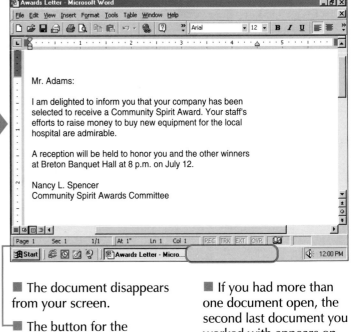

■ To save the document displayed on your screen before closing, see page 22.

1 Click **File**.

2 Click **Close** to close the document.

■ The document disappears from your screen.

■ The button for the document disappears from the taskbar.

■ If you had more than one document open, the second last document you worked with appears on your screen.

EXIT WORD

When you finish
using Word, you can
exit the program.

You should always
exit all programs
before turning off
your computer.

EXIT WORD

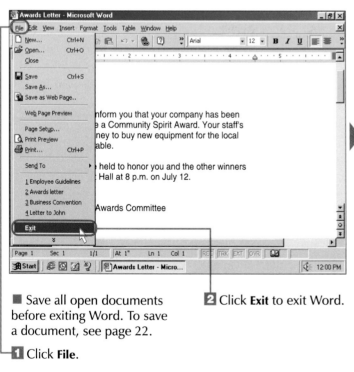

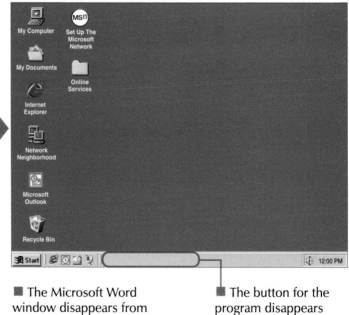

■ Save all open documents
before exiting Word. To save
a document, see page 22.

1 Click **File**.

2 Click **Exit** to exit Word.

■ The Microsoft Word
window disappears from
your screen.

■ The button for the
program disappears
from the taskbar.

You can open a saved document and display it on your screen. This allows you to review and make changes to the document.

OPEN A DOCUMENT

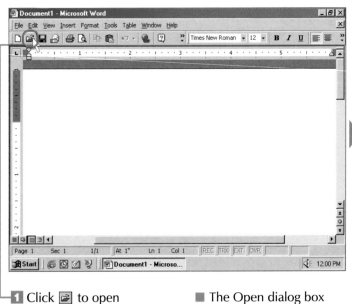

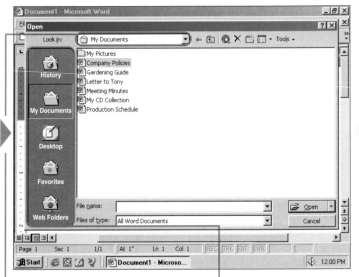

1 Click 📂 to open a document.

Note: If 📂 is not displayed, click ⏵ on the Standard toolbar to display all the buttons.

■ The Open dialog box appears.

■ This area shows the location of the displayed documents. You can click this area to change the location.

■ This area allows you to access commonly used folders. To display the contents of a folder, click the folder.

Note: For information on the commonly used folders, see the top of page 23.

26

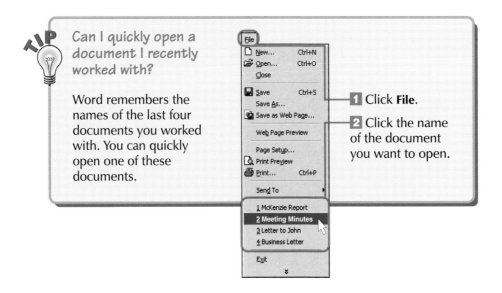

TIP

Can I quickly open a document I recently worked with?

Word remembers the names of the last four documents you worked with. You can quickly open one of these documents.

1 Click **File**.

2 Click the name of the document you want to open.

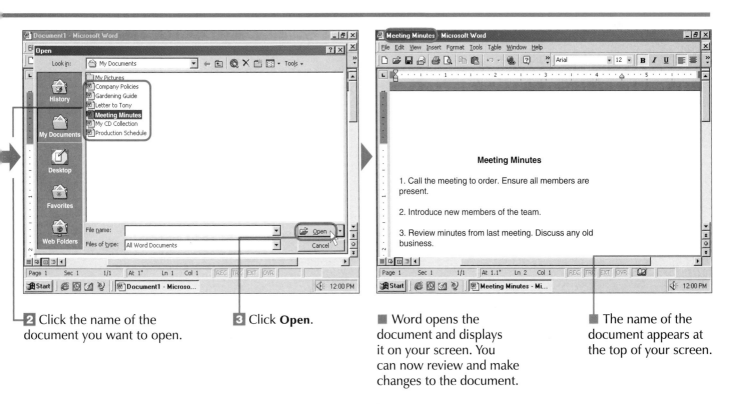

2 Click the name of the document you want to open.

3 Click **Open**.

■ Word opens the document and displays it on your screen. You can now review and make changes to the document.

■ The name of the document appears at the top of your screen.

FIND A DOCUMENT

If you cannot remember the name or location of a document you want to work with, you can search for the document.

FIND A DOCUMENT

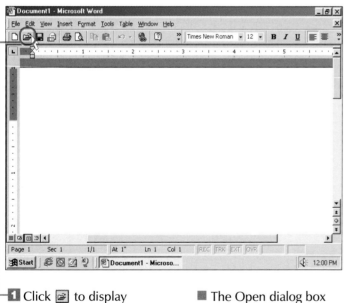

1 Click 📂 to display the Open dialog box.

Note: If 📂 is not displayed, click ⁇ on the Standard toolbar to display all the buttons.

■ The Open dialog box appears.

2 Click **Tools**.

3 Click **Find**.

■ The Find dialog box appears.

How can I search for a document?

When searching for a document, you must specify a property for the search. Common properties include the document contents, creation date, file name and number of pages. After you specify a property, you can specify a condition and value for the search.

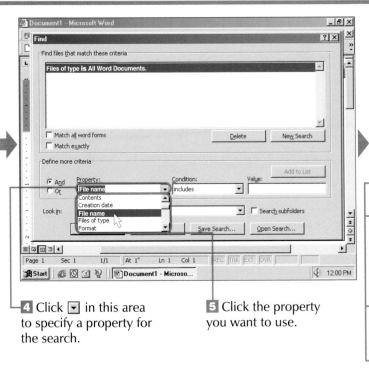

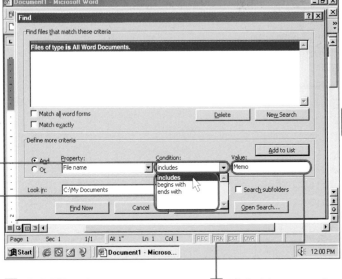

4 Click ▾ in this area to specify a property for the search.

5 Click the property you want to use.

6 Click ▾ in this area to specify a condition for the search.

7 Click the condition you want to use.

Note: The available conditions depend on the property you selected in step 5.

8 Click this area and type the value you want to search for.

Note: If the value area is not available, you do not need to enter a value.

CONTINUED

FIND A DOCUMENT

You can specify the location where you want to search for a document.

FIND A DOCUMENT (CONTINUED)

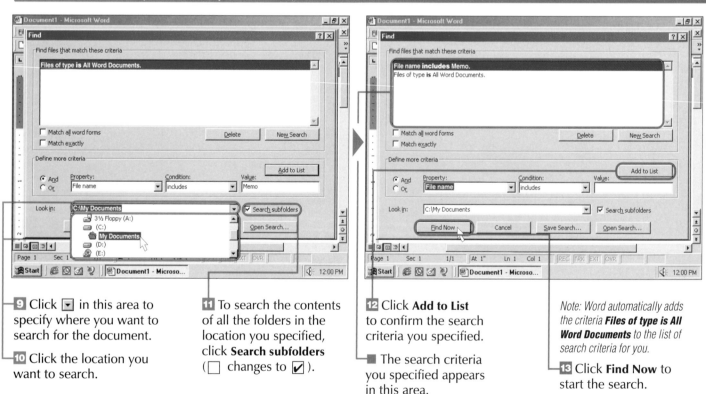

-9 Click ▾ in this area to specify where you want to search for the document.

-10 Click the location you want to search.

11 To search the contents of all the folders in the location you specified, click **Search subfolders** (☐ changes to ☑).

12 Click **Add to List** to confirm the search criteria you specified.

■ The search criteria you specified appears in this area.

Note: Word automatically adds the criteria Files of type is All Word Documents to the list of search criteria for you.

-13 Click **Find Now** to start the search.

When I started the search, why did a dialog box appear, asking if I want to install FindFast?

FindFast is a feature that can help speed up your searches. To install FindFast, insert the CD-ROM disc you used to install Word into your CD-ROM drive. Then click **Yes** to install FindFast.

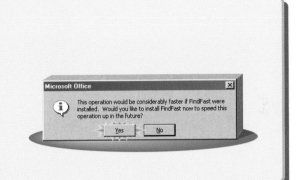

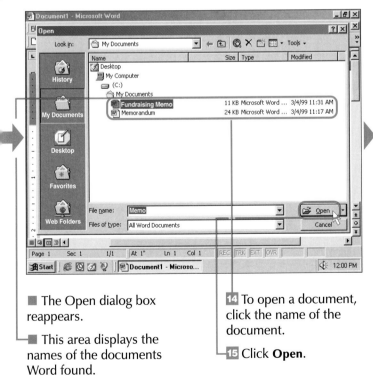

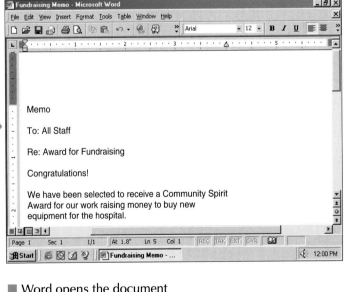

■ The Open dialog box reappears.

■ This area displays the names of the documents Word found.

14 To open a document, click the name of the document.

15 Click **Open**.

■ Word opens the document and displays it on your screen. You can now review and make changes to the document.

CHAPTER 3

CHANGE DISPLAY OF DOCUMENTS

Would you like to change the way your document appears on your screen? In this chapter you will learn how to display your document in a different view, zoom in or out, display or hide a toolbar and more.

CHANGE THE VIEW

Word offers four ways to view your document. You can choose the view that best suits your needs.

VIEWS

- ☐ Normal
- ☐ Web Layout
- ☑ Print Layout
- ☐ Outline

CHANGE THE VIEW

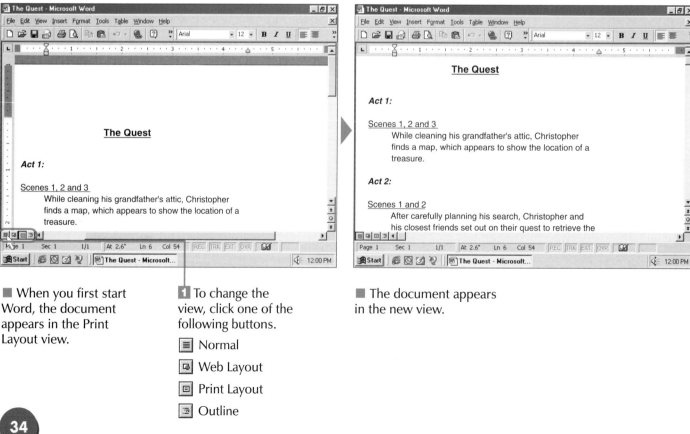

■ When you first start Word, the document appears in the Print Layout view.

1 To change the view, click one of the following buttons.

≣ Normal

🔲 Web Layout

🔲 Print Layout

🔲 Outline

■ The document appears in the new view.

THE FOUR VIEWS

Normal View

This view simplifies your document so you can quickly enter, edit and format text. The Normal view does not display margins, headers, footers or page numbers.

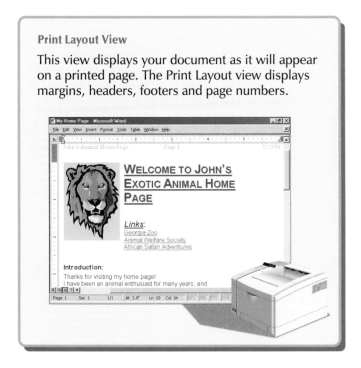

Web Layout View

This view displays your document as it will appear on the Web. The Web Layout view is useful when you are using Word to create a Web page.

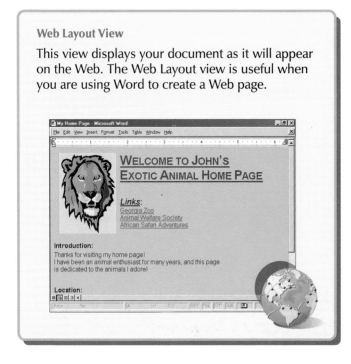

Print Layout View

This view displays your document as it will appear on a printed page. The Print Layout view displays margins, headers, footers and page numbers.

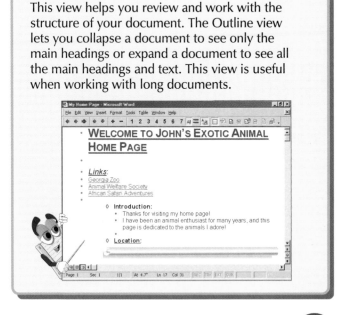

Outline View

This view helps you review and work with the structure of your document. The Outline view lets you collapse a document to see only the main headings or expand a document to see all the main headings and text. This view is useful when working with long documents.

Word allows you to enlarge or reduce the display of text on your screen.

Changing the zoom setting will not affect the way text appears on a printed page.

ZOOM IN OR OUT

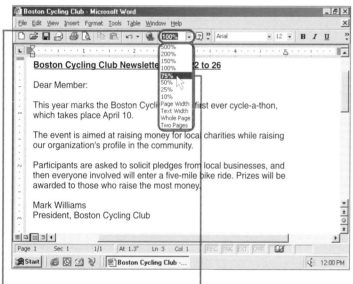

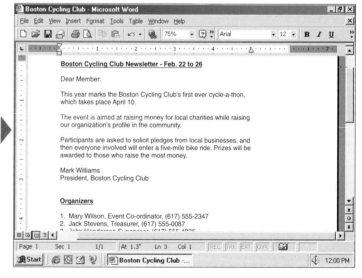

1 Click ▼ in this area to display a list of zoom settings.

Note: If the Zoom area is not displayed, click ▸ on the Standard toolbar to display all the buttons.

2 Click the zoom setting you want to use.

■ The document appears in the new zoom setting. You can edit the document as usual.

■ To return to the normal zoom setting, repeat steps **1** and **2**, except select **100%** in step **2**.

DISPLAY OR HIDE THE RULER

You can display or hide the ruler at any time. The ruler helps you position text in a document.

When you first start Word, the ruler appears on your screen. Hiding the ruler provides a larger and less cluttered working area.

You cannot display or hide the ruler in the Outline view. For more information on the views, see page 34.

DISPLAY OR HIDE THE RULER

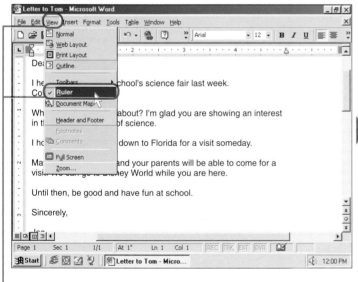

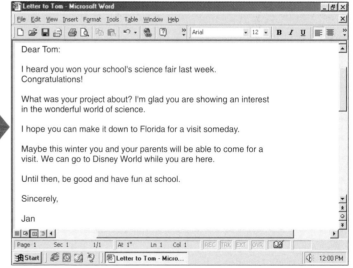

1 Click **View**.

2 Click **Ruler**. A check mark (✔) beside **Ruler** indicates the ruler is currently displayed.

Note: If Ruler does not appear on the menu, position the mouse ⌖ over the bottom of the menu to display all the menu commands.

■ Word displays or hides the ruler.

DISPLAY OR HIDE A TOOLBAR

Word offers several toolbars that you can display or hide at any time. Each toolbar contains buttons that help you quickly perform common tasks.

You can choose which toolbars to display based on the tasks you perform most often.

DISPLAY OR HIDE A TOOLBAR

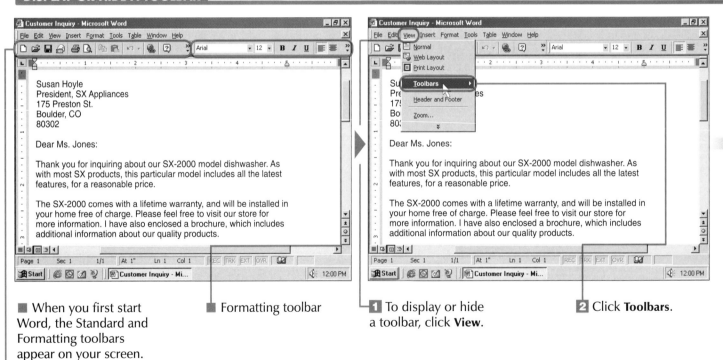

■ When you first start Word, the Standard and Formatting toolbars appear on your screen.

■ Standard toolbar

■ Formatting toolbar

1 To display or hide a toolbar, click **View**.

2 Click **Toolbars**.

38

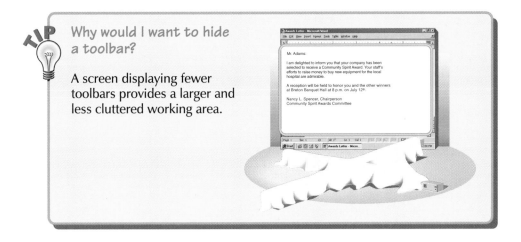

Why would I want to hide a toolbar?

A screen displaying fewer toolbars provides a larger and less cluttered working area.

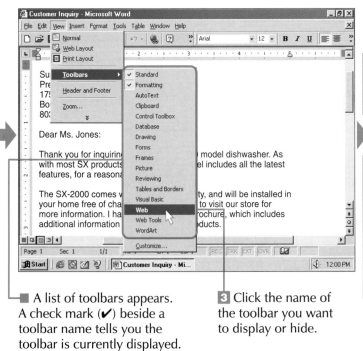

■ A list of toolbars appears. A check mark (✔) beside a toolbar name tells you the toolbar is currently displayed.

3 Click the name of the toolbar you want to display or hide.

■ Word displays or hides the toolbar you selected.

You can increase the size of a toolbar to display more buttons on the toolbar. This is useful when a toolbar appears on the same row as another toolbar and cannot display all of its buttons.

You cannot size a toolbar that appears on its own row.

SIZE A TOOLBAR

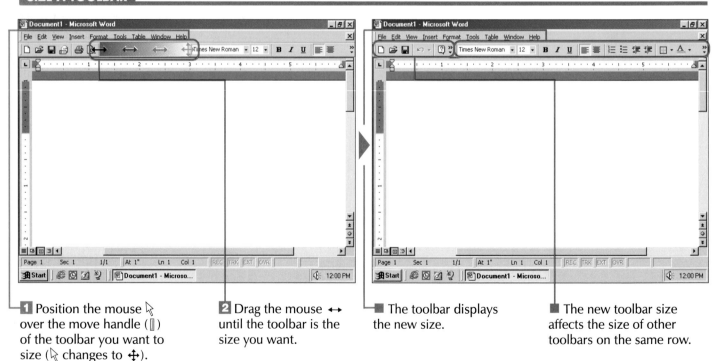

1 Position the mouse ⌖ over the move handle (▯) of the toolbar you want to size (⌖ changes to ✛).

2 Drag the mouse ↔ until the toolbar is the size you want.

■ The toolbar displays the new size.

■ The new toolbar size affects the size of other toolbars on the same row.

MOVE A TOOLBAR

You can move a toolbar to the top, bottom, right or left edge of your screen.

Moving a toolbar to its own row allows you to display more buttons on the toolbar.

MOVE A TOOLBAR

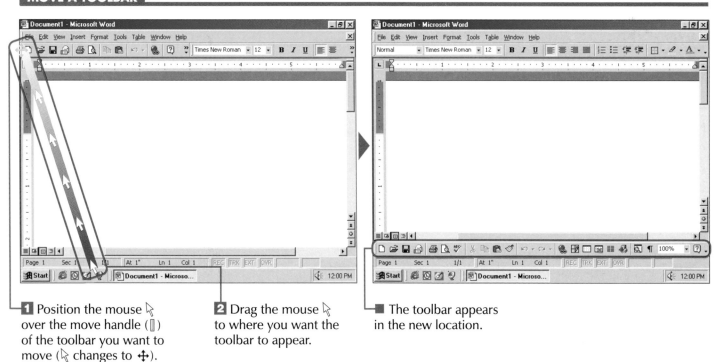

1 Position the mouse ⌖ over the move handle (▯) of the toolbar you want to move (⌖ changes to ✛).

2 Drag the mouse ⌖ to where you want the toolbar to appear.

■ The toolbar appears in the new location.

41

CHAPTER 4

EDIT TEXT

Do you want to edit the text in your document or check your document for spelling and grammar errors? This chapter teaches you how.

INSERT AND DELETE TEXT

Word lets you add new text to your document and remove text you no longer need.

INSERT TEXT

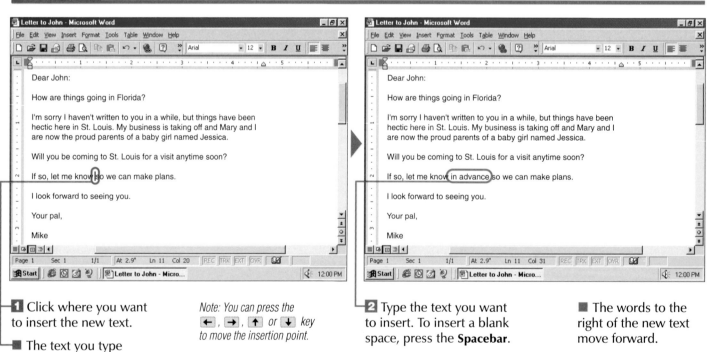

1 Click where you want to insert the new text.

■ The text you type will appear where the insertion point flashes on your screen.

Note: You can press the ←, →, ↑ or ↓ key to move the insertion point.

2 Type the text you want to insert. To insert a blank space, press the **Spacebar**.

■ The words to the right of the new text move forward.

TIP

Why does the existing text in my document disappear when I insert new text?

When **OVR** appears in **bold** at the bottom of your screen, the Overtype feature is on. When this feature is on, the text you type will replace the existing text in your document. To turn off the Overtype feature, press the `Insert` key.

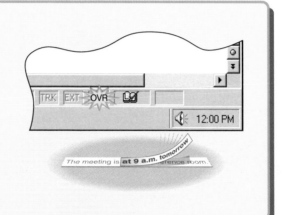

DELETE TEXT

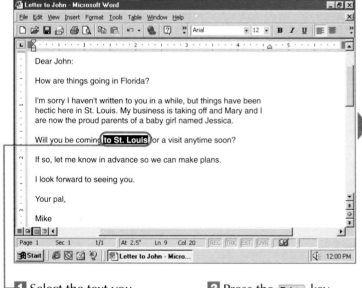

1 Select the text you want to delete. To select text, see page 14.

2 Press the `Delete` key to remove the text.

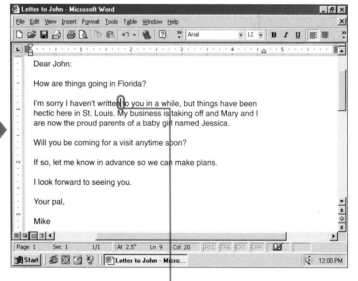

■ The text disappears. The remaining text moves to fill any empty spaces.

DELETE ONE CHARACTER

1 Click to the right of the character you want to delete.

2 Press the `Backspace` key to delete the character to the left of the flashing insertion point.

45

You can insert the current date and time into your document. Word can automatically update the date and time each time you open or print the document.

Press Release
From: Earth Wise Enterprises

Sales of tree planting kits will aid environmental group.

Earth Wise Enterprises announced today that it has expanded its worldwide mail order service to include the sale of tree planting kits. Fifty cents from the sale of each kit will be donated to the World Reforestation Fund, a nonprofit organization dedicated to increasing the size and number of forests around the world.

9/15/99 1:58 PM

INSERT THE DATE AND TIME

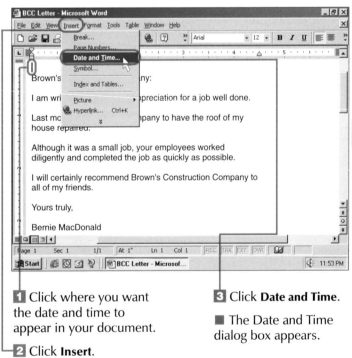

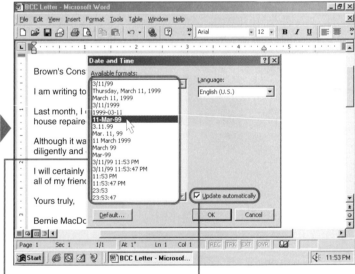

1 Click where you want the date and time to appear in your document.

2 Click **Insert**.

3 Click **Date and Time**.

■ The Date and Time dialog box appears.

4 Click the date and time format you want to use.

5 When this option displays a check mark (☑), Word will automatically update the date and time each time you open or print the document. You can click the option to add (☑) or remove (☐) the check mark.

TIP

Why did Word insert the wrong date and time into my document?

Word uses your computer's built-in clock to determine the current date and time. If Word inserts the wrong date and time into your document, you must change the date and time set in your computer. To change the date and time set in your computer, refer to your Windows manual.

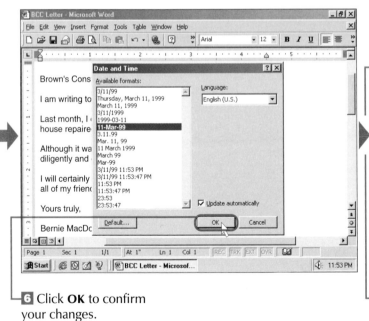

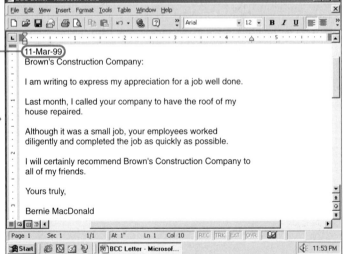

6 Click **OK** to confirm your changes.

■ The date and time format you selected appears in your document.

You can move or copy text to a new location in your document by dragging and dropping the text. This method is useful when moving or copying text short distances in your document.

USING DRAG AND DROP

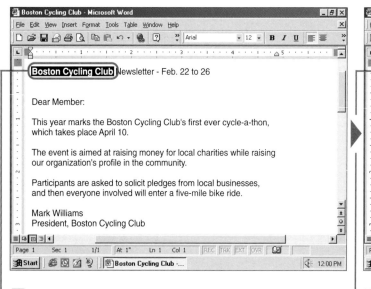

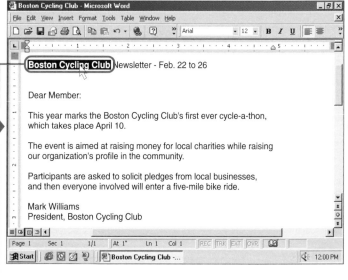

1 Select the text you want to move or copy. To select text, see page 14.

2 Position the mouse I over the selected text (I changes to).

What is the difference between moving and copying text?

Moving text

Moving text allows you to rearrange text in your document. When you move text, the text disappears from its original location in your document.

Copying text

Copying text allows you to repeat information in your document without having to retype the text. When you copy text, the text appears in both the original and new locations.

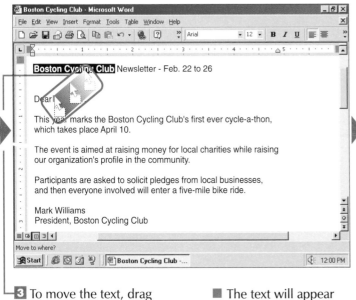

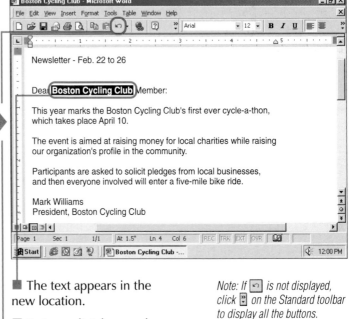

3 To move the text, drag the mouse ⬚ to where you want to place the text.

■ To copy the text, press and hold down the **Ctrl** key as you drag the mouse ⬚ to where you want to place the text.

■ The text will appear where you position the dotted insertion point on your screen.

■ The text appears in the new location.

■ To immediately cancel the move or copy, click ⟲.

Note: If ⟲ is not displayed, click ⟩ on the Standard toolbar to display all the buttons.

MOVE OR COPY TEXT

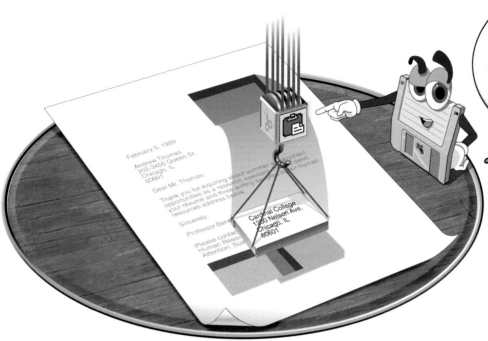

You can move or copy text to a new location in your document by using toolbar buttons. This method is useful when moving or copying text long distances in your document.

USING THE TOOLBAR BUTTONS

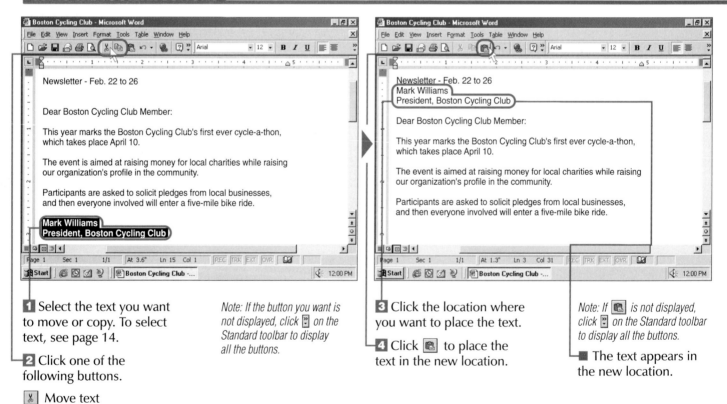

1 Select the text you want to move or copy. To select text, see page 14.

2 Click one of the following buttons.

✂ Move text

📋 Copy text

Note: If the button you want is not displayed, click » *on the Standard toolbar to display all the buttons.*

3 Click the location where you want to place the text.

4 Click 📋 to place the text in the new location.

Note: If 📋 *is not displayed, click* » *on the Standard toolbar to display all the buttons.*

■ The text appears in the new location.

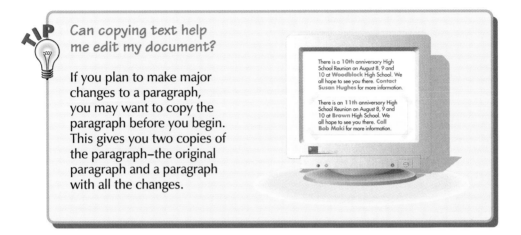

TIP

Can copying text help me edit my document?

If you plan to make major changes to a paragraph, you may want to copy the paragraph before you begin. This gives you two copies of the paragraph–the original paragraph and a paragraph with all the changes.

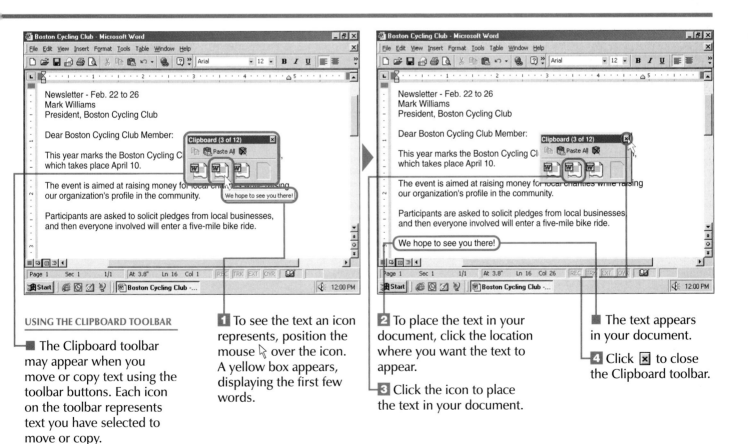

USING THE CLIPBOARD TOOLBAR

■ The Clipboard toolbar may appear when you move or copy text using the toolbar buttons. Each icon on the toolbar represents text you have selected to move or copy.

Note: To display the Clipboard toolbar, see page 38.

1 To see the text an icon represents, position the mouse ⌖ over the icon. A yellow box appears, displaying the first few words.

2 To place the text in your document, click the location where you want the text to appear.

3 Click the icon to place the text in your document.

■ The text appears in your document.

4 Click ⊠ to close the Clipboard toolbar.

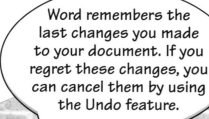

Word remembers the last changes you made to your document. If you regret these changes, you can cancel them by using the Undo feature.

The Undo feature can cancel your last editing and formatting changes.

UNDO CHANGES

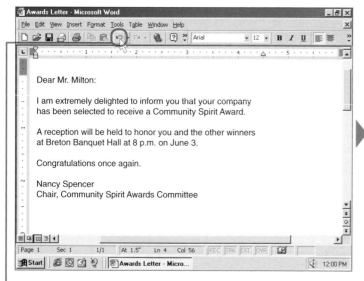

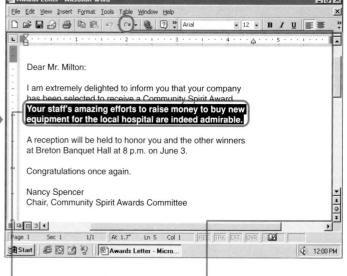

1 Click 🔄 to undo the last change you made to your document.

Note: If 🔄 is not displayed, click 🔽 on the Standard toolbar to display all the buttons.

■ Word cancels the last change you made to your document.

■ You can repeat step **1** to cancel previous changes you made.

■ To reverse the results of using the Undo feature, click 🔄.

Note: If 🔄 is not displayed, click 🔽 on the Standard toolbar to display all the buttons.

COUNT WORDS IN A DOCUMENT

You can quickly count the number of words in your document.

Dear Susan:

Trafalgar High School celebrates its 50th anniversary this year. We will be celebrating on September 11th with an Open House, followed by a buffet dinner.

Please bring your school photos and memorabilia for our display table.

Word Count

When you count the number of words in your document, Word also displays the number of pages, characters, paragraphs and lines in the document.

COUNT WORDS IN A DOCUMENT

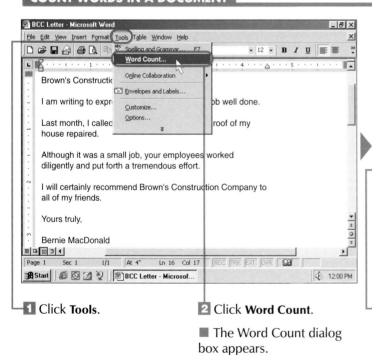

1 Click **Tools**.

2 Click **Word Count**.

■ The Word Count dialog box appears.

■ This area displays information about your document, including the total number of words in the document.

3 When you finish reviewing the information, click **Close** to close the Word Count dialog box.

You can use the Find feature to locate a word or phrase in your document.

FIND TEXT

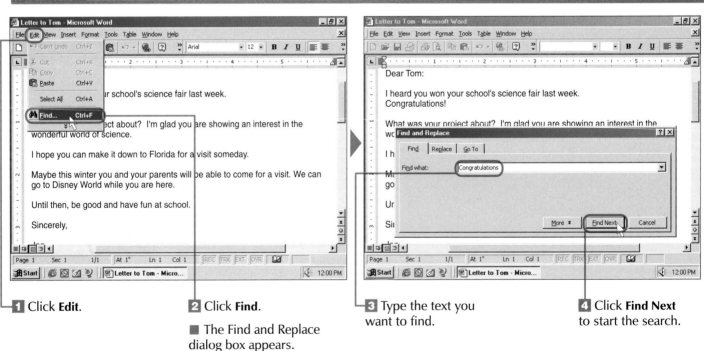

1 Click **Edit**.

2 Click **Find**.

■ The Find and Replace dialog box appears.

3 Type the text you want to find.

4 Click **Find Next** to start the search.

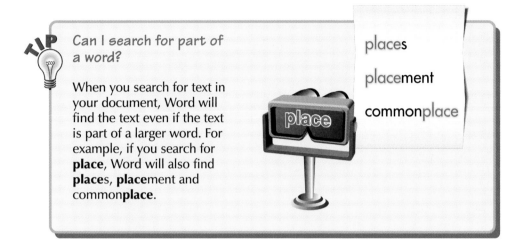

Can I search for part of a word?

When you search for text in your document, Word will find the text even if the text is part of a larger word. For example, if you search for **place**, Word will also find **place**s, **place**ment and common**place**.

places

placement

commonplace

place

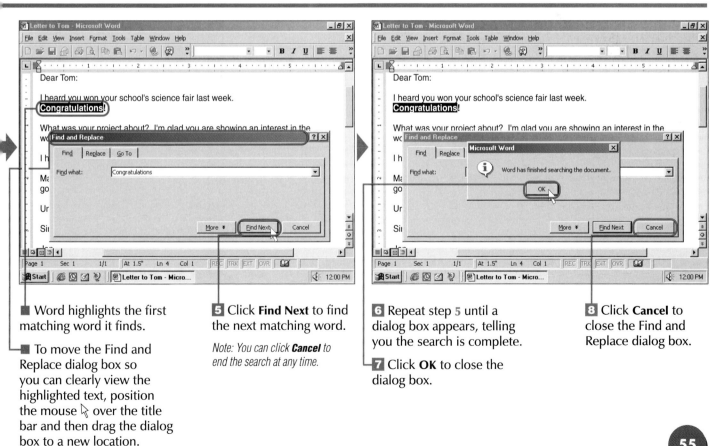

■ Word highlights the first matching word it finds.

■ To move the Find and Replace dialog box so you can clearly view the highlighted text, position the mouse ⌇ over the title bar and then drag the dialog box to a new location.

5 Click **Find Next** to find the next matching word.

*Note: You can click **Cancel** to end the search at any time.*

6 Repeat step 5 until a dialog box appears, telling you the search is complete.

7 Click **OK** to close the dialog box.

8 Click **Cancel** to close the Find and Replace dialog box.

REPLACE TEXT

The Replace feature can locate and replace every occurrence of a word or phrase in your document. This is useful if you have frequently misspelled a name.

REPLACE TEXT

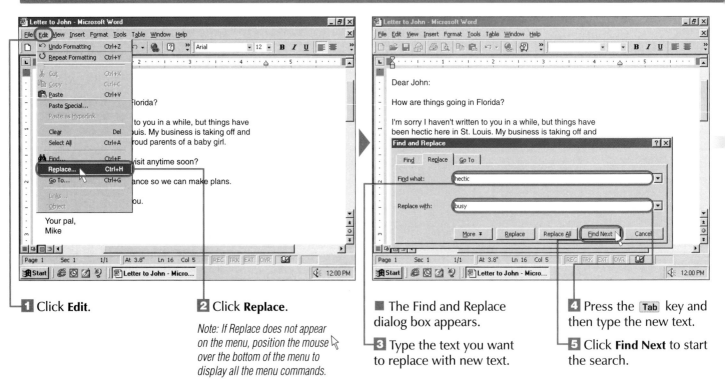

1 Click **Edit**.

2 Click **Replace**.

Note: If Replace does not appear on the menu, position the mouse over the bottom of the menu to display all the menu commands.

■ The Find and Replace dialog box appears.

3 Type the text you want to replace with new text.

4 Press the Tab key and then type the new text.

5 Click **Find Next** to start the search.

56

Can I use the Replace feature to quickly enter text?

The Replace feature is useful when you have to type a long word or phrase, such as **University of Massachusetts**, many times in a document.

You can type a short form of the word or phrase, such as **UM**, throughout your document and then have Word replace the short form with the full word or phrase.

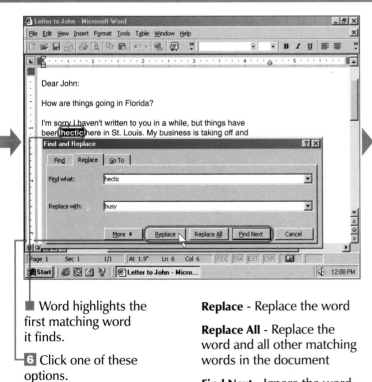

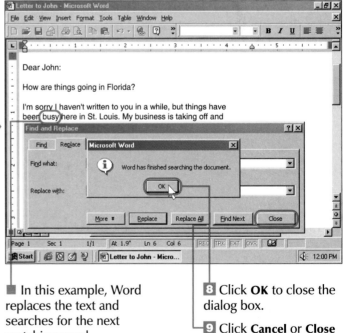

■ Word highlights the first matching word it finds.

6 Click one of these options.

Replace - Replace the word

Replace All - Replace the word and all other matching words in the document

Find Next - Ignore the word

*Note: To end the search at any time, click **Cancel**.*

■ In this example, Word replaces the text and searches for the next matching word.

7 Repeat step 6 until a dialog box appears, telling you the search is complete.

8 Click **OK** to close the dialog box.

9 Click **Cancel** or **Close** to close the Find and Replace dialog box.

CHECK SPELLING AND GRAMMAR

Word automatically checks your document for spelling and grammar errors as you type. You can correct the errors that Word finds.

CORRECT AN ERROR

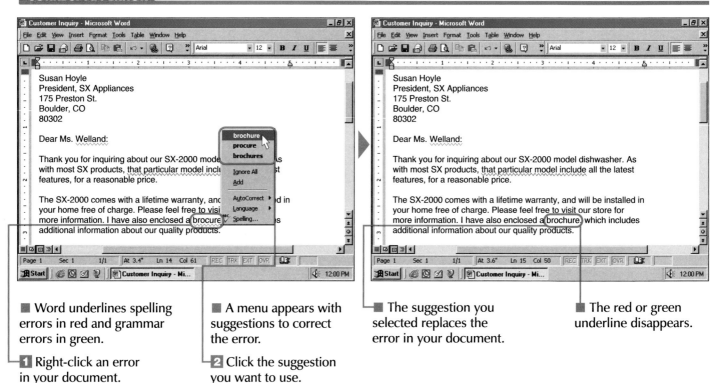

■ Word underlines spelling errors in red and grammar errors in green.

1 Right-click an error in your document.

■ A menu appears with suggestions to correct the error.

2 Click the suggestion you want to use.

Note: If Word does not display a suggestion you want to use, click outside the menu to close the menu.

■ The suggestion you selected replaces the error in your document.

■ The red or green underline disappears.

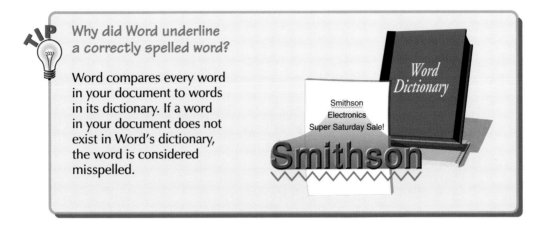

TIP

Why did Word underline a correctly spelled word?

Word compares every word in your document to words in its dictionary. If a word in your document does not exist in Word's dictionary, the word is considered misspelled.

IGNORE AN ERROR

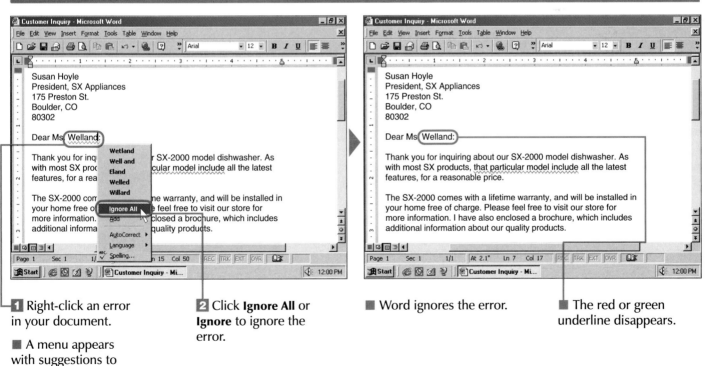

1 Right-click an error in your document.

■ A menu appears with suggestions to correct the error.

2 Click **Ignore All** or **Ignore** to ignore the error.

■ Word ignores the error.

■ The red or green underline disappears.

CHECK SPELLING AND GRAMMAR

You can find and correct all the spelling and grammar errors in your document at once.

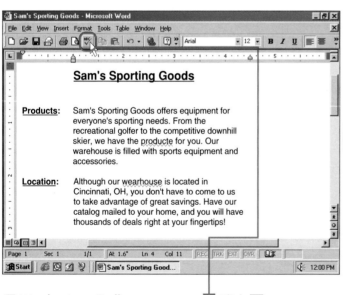

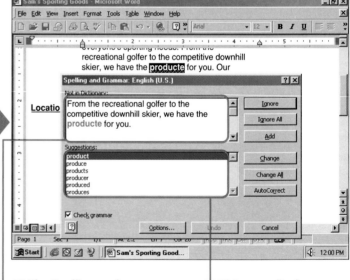

■ Word automatically underlines spelling errors in red and grammar errors in green.

1 Click 🔤 to correct your entire document.

Note: If 🔤 is not displayed, click 🔀 on the Standard toolbar to display all the buttons.

■ The Spelling and Grammar dialog box appears if Word finds an error in your document.

■ This area displays the spelling or grammar error.

■ This area displays suggestions for correcting the error.

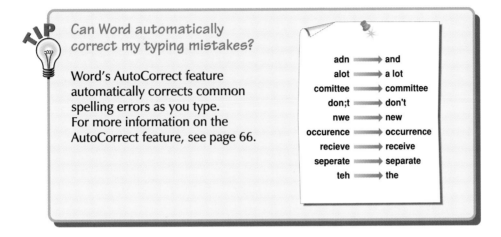

Can Word automatically correct my typing mistakes?

Word's AutoCorrect feature automatically corrects common spelling errors as you type. For more information on the AutoCorrect feature, see page 66.

adn ⟹	and
alot ⟹	a lot
comittee ⟹	committee
don;t ⟹	don't
nwe ⟹	new
occurence ⟹	occurrence
recieve ⟹	receive
seperate ⟹	separate
teh ⟹	the

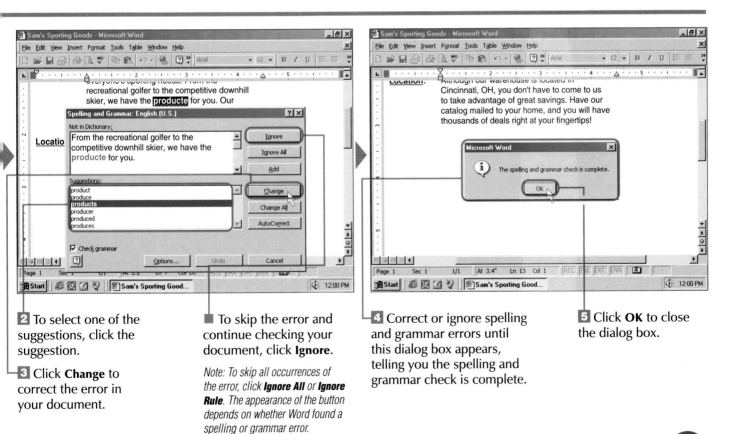

2 To select one of the suggestions, click the suggestion.

3 Click **Change** to correct the error in your document.

■ To skip the error and continue checking your document, click **Ignore**.

*Note: To skip all occurrences of the error, click **Ignore All** or **Ignore Rule**. The appearance of the button depends on whether Word found a spelling or grammar error.*

4 Correct or ignore spelling and grammar errors until this dialog box appears, telling you the spelling and grammar check is complete.

5 Click **OK** to close the dialog box.

You can use the Thesaurus feature to replace a word in your document with a word that is more suitable.

USING THE THESAURUS

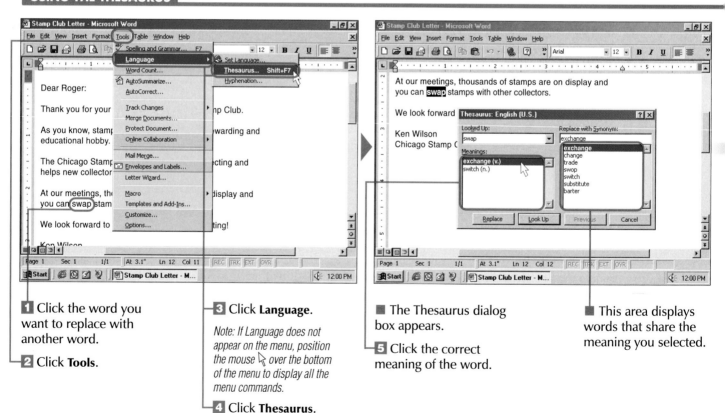

1 Click the word you want to replace with another word.

2 Click **Tools**.

3 Click **Language**.

Note: If Language does not appear on the menu, position the mouse over the bottom of the menu to display all the menu commands.

4 Click **Thesaurus**.

■ The Thesaurus dialog box appears.

5 Click the correct meaning of the word.

■ This area displays words that share the meaning you selected.

How can the thesaurus help me?

Many people use the thesaurus to replace a word that appears repeatedly in a document. Replacing repeatedly used words can help add variety to your writing. Using the thesaurus included with Word is faster and more convenient than searching through a printed thesaurus.

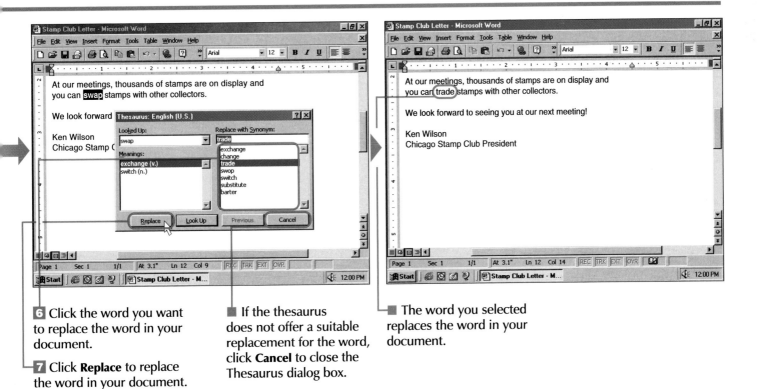

6 Click the word you want to replace the word in your document.

7 Click **Replace** to replace the word in your document.

■ If the thesaurus does not offer a suitable replacement for the word, click **Cancel** to close the Thesaurus dialog box.

■ The word you selected replaces the word in your document.

You can insert symbols that do not appear on your keyboard into your document.

INSERT SYMBOLS

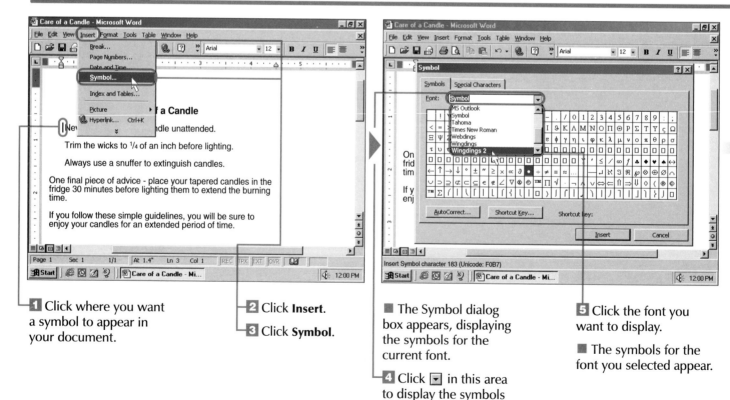

1 Click where you want a symbol to appear in your document.

2 Click **Insert**.

3 Click **Symbol**.

■ The Symbol dialog box appears, displaying the symbols for the current font.

4 Click ▼ in this area to display the symbols for another font.

5 Click the font you want to display.

■ The symbols for the font you selected appear.

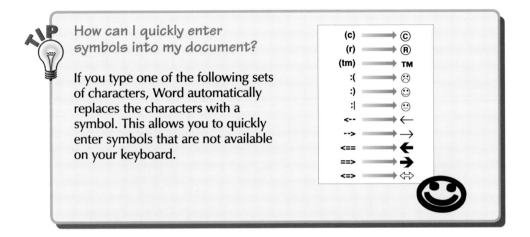

TIP

How can I quickly enter symbols into my document?

If you type one of the following sets of characters, Word automatically replaces the characters with a symbol. This allows you to quickly enter symbols that are not available on your keyboard.

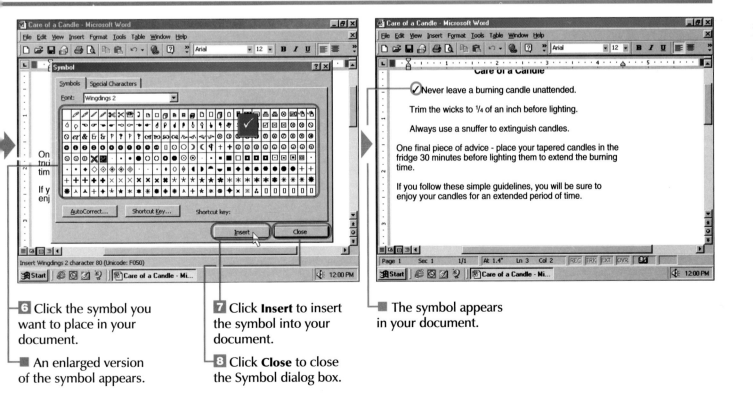

■ **6** Click the symbol you want to place in your document.

■ An enlarged version of the symbol appears.

■ **7** Click **Insert** to insert the symbol into your document.

■ **8** Click **Close** to close the Symbol dialog box.

■ The symbol appears in your document.

USING AUTOCORRECT

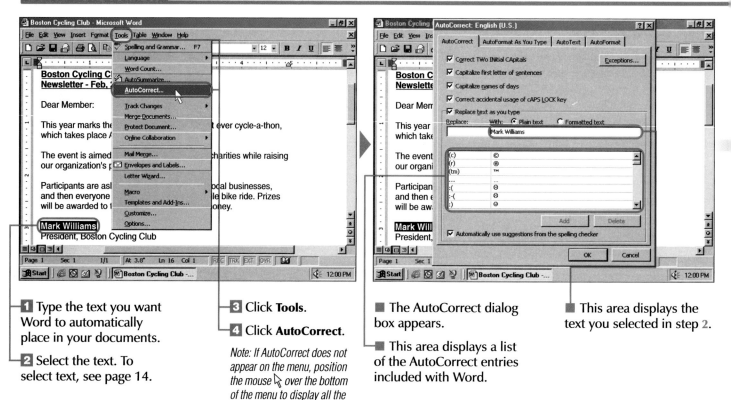

1 Type the text you want Word to automatically place in your documents.

2 Select the text. To select text, see page 14.

3 Click **Tools**.

4 Click **AutoCorrect**.

Note: If AutoCorrect does not appear on the menu, position the mouse ⌖ over the bottom of the menu to display all the menu commands.

■ The AutoCorrect dialog box appears.

■ This area displays a list of the AutoCorrect entries included with Word.

■ This area displays the text you selected in step 2.

TIP

What types of AutoCorrect entries can I create?

You can create AutoCorrect entries for typing, spelling and grammar errors you often make. You can also create AutoCorrect entries to quickly enter words and phrases you frequently use, such as your name.

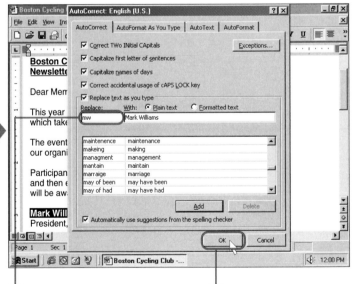

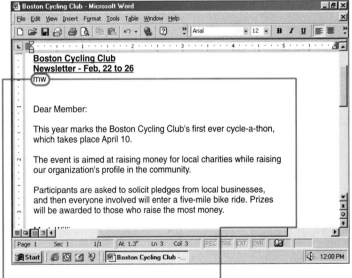

5 Type the text you want Word to replace automatically with the text you selected in step **2**. The text should not contain spaces and should not be a real word.

6 Click **OK** to confirm your changes.

INSERT AN AUTOCORRECT ENTRY

■ After you create an AutoCorrect entry, Word will automatically insert the entry each time you type the corresponding text.

1 Click where you want the AutoCorrect entry to appear in your document.

2 Type the text Word will automatically replace.

3 Press the **Spacebar** and the AutoCorrect entry replaces the text you typed.

USING AUTOTEXT

You can use the AutoText feature to store text you frequently use. This lets you avoid typing the same information over and over again.

Dear Susan:

Trafalgar High School celebrates its 50th anniversary this year. We will be celebrating on September 11th with an Open House, followed by a buffet dinner.

Please bring your school photos and memorabilia for our display table.

Becky Flynn
Social Committee

CREATE AN AUTOTEXT ENTRY

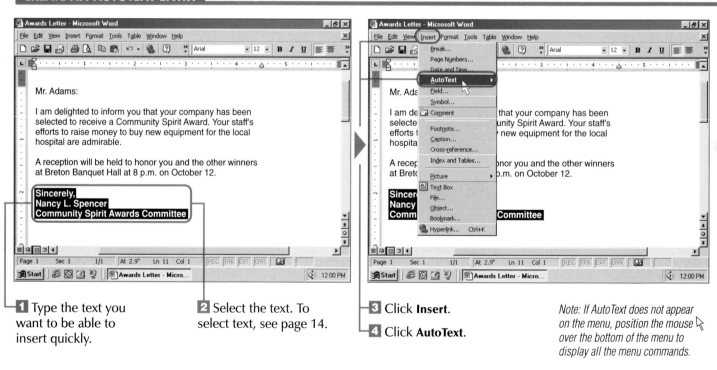

1 Type the text you want to be able to insert quickly.

2 Select the text. To select text, see page 14.

3 Click **Insert**.

4 Click **AutoText**.

Note: If AutoText does not appear on the menu, position the mouse over the bottom of the menu to display all the menu commands.

What types of AutoText entries can I create?

You can create an AutoText entry for information you plan to use often, such as a mailing address, product name, legal disclaimer or closing remark. Word will store any formatting you apply to the text, such as bold or underline. To format text, see pages 74 to 83.

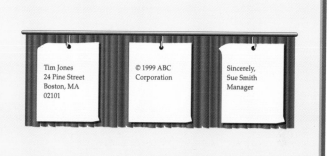

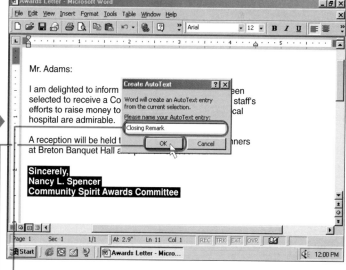

5 Click **New**.

■ The Create AutoText dialog box appears.

6 This area displays a name for the AutoText entry. To use a different name, type the name.

7 Click **OK** to create the AutoText entry.

■ You can now use the AutoText entry in all of your documents. To insert the AutoText entry into a document, see page 70.

> After you create an AutoText entry, you can insert the text into a document.

INSERT AN AUTOTEXT ENTRY

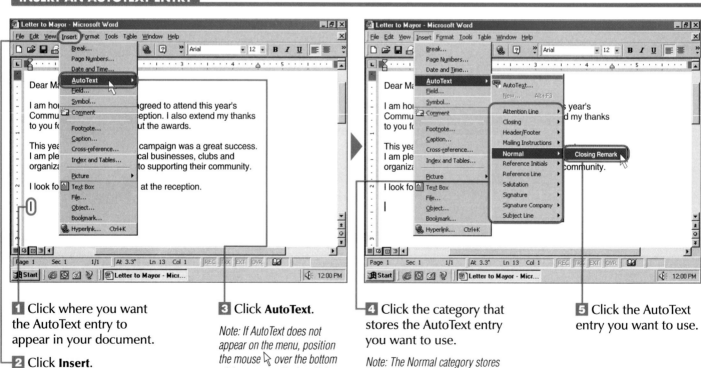

1 Click where you want the AutoText entry to appear in your document.

2 Click **Insert**.

3 Click **AutoText**.

Note: If AutoText does not appear on the menu, position the mouse ↕ over the bottom of the menu to display all the menu commands.

4 Click the category that stores the AutoText entry you want to use.

Note: The Normal category stores most AutoText entries you have created.

5 Click the AutoText entry you want to use.

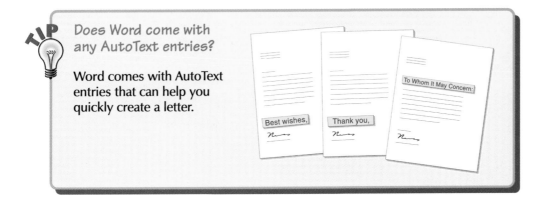

Does Word come with any AutoText entries?

Word comes with AutoText entries that can help you quickly create a letter.

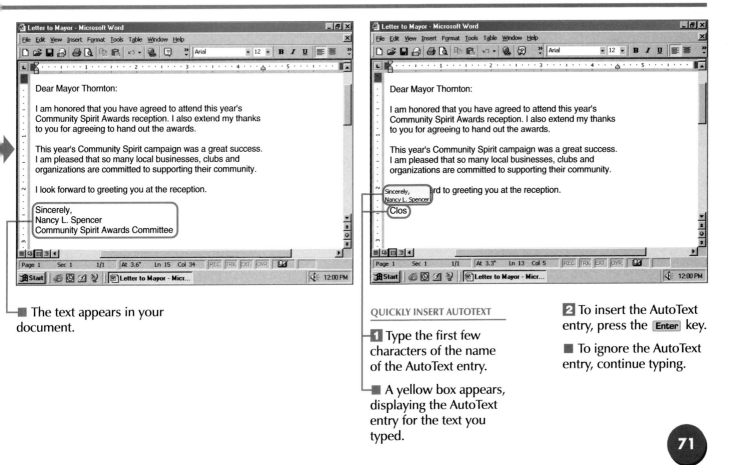

■ The text appears in your document.

QUICKLY INSERT AUTOTEXT

1 Type the first few characters of the name of the AutoText entry.

■ A yellow box appears, displaying the AutoText entry for the text you typed.

2 To insert the AutoText entry, press the Enter key.

■ To ignore the AutoText entry, continue typing.

CHAPTER 5

FORMAT TEXT

Would you like to emphasize information in your document and enhance the appearance of text? Read this chapter to learn how.

DEAR MRS. GLEDHILL:

There is a 10th anni

School Reuni

and 8

BOLD, ITALICIZE OR UNDERLINE TEXT

You can use the Bold, Italic and Underline features to emphasize text in your document.

BOLD, ITALICIZE OR UNDERLINE TEXT

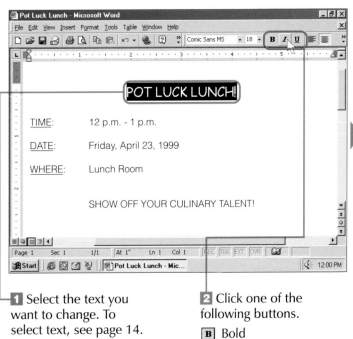

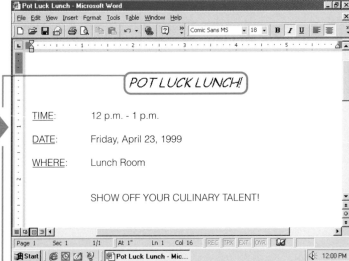

1 Select the text you want to change. To select text, see page 14.

2 Click one of the following buttons.

B Bold

I Italic

U Underline

Note: If the button you want is not displayed, click ⟫ on the Formatting toolbar to display all the buttons.

■ The text you selected appears in the new style.

■ To deselect text, click outside the selected area.

■ To remove a bold, italic or underline style, repeat steps 1 and 2.

CHANGE CASE OF TEXT

You can change the case of text in your document without retyping the text. Word offers five case styles you can choose from.

CHANGE CASE OF TEXT

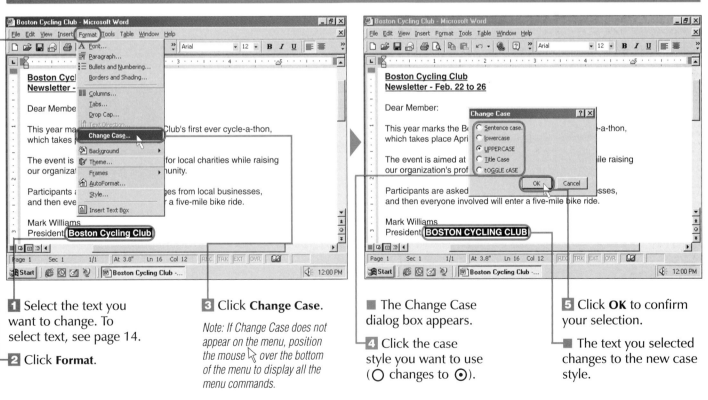

1 Select the text you want to change. To select text, see page 14.

2 Click **Format**.

3 Click **Change Case**.

Note: If Change Case does not appear on the menu, position the mouse ⟍ over the bottom of the menu to display all the menu commands.

■ The Change Case dialog box appears.

4 Click the case style you want to use (○ changes to ◉).

5 Click **OK** to confirm your selection.

■ The text you selected changes to the new case style.

You can enhance the appearance of your document by changing the design, or font, of the text.

CHANGE FONT OF TEXT

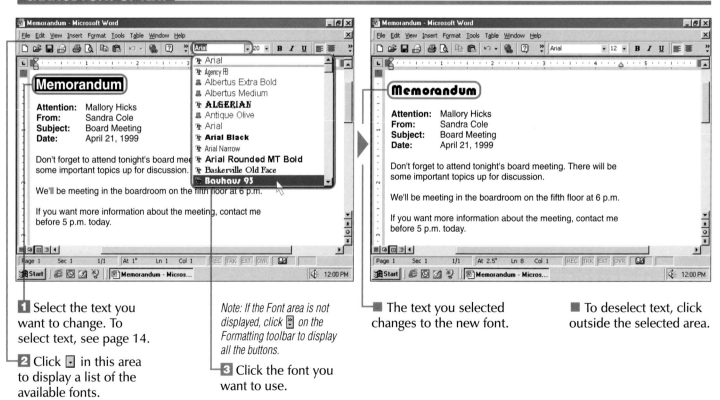

1 Select the text you want to change. To select text, see page 14.

2 Click ⬛ in this area to display a list of the available fonts.

Note: If the Font area is not displayed, click ⬛ on the Formatting toolbar to display all the buttons.

3 Click the font you want to use.

■ The text you selected changes to the new font.

■ To deselect text, click outside the selected area.

CHANGE SIZE OF TEXT

You can increase or decrease the size of text in your document.

Word measures the size of text in points. There are approximately 72 points in one inch.

Larger text is easier to read, but smaller text allows you to fit more information on a page.

CHANGE SIZE OF TEXT

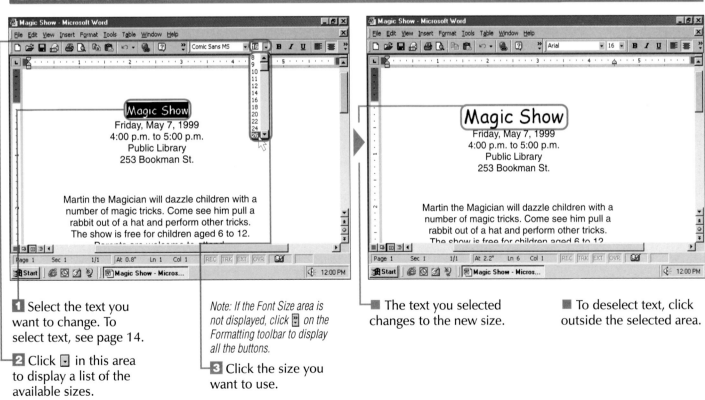

1 Select the text you want to change. To select text, see page 14.

2 Click ☐ in this area to display a list of the available sizes.

Note: If the Font Size area is not displayed, click ☒ on the Formatting toolbar to display all the buttons.

3 Click the size you want to use.

■ The text you selected changes to the new size.

■ To deselect text, click outside the selected area.

> You can change the color of text to draw attention to headings or important information in your document.

CHANGE COLOR OF TEXT

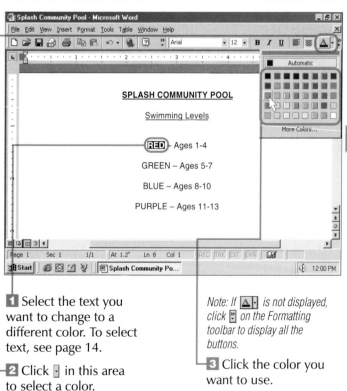

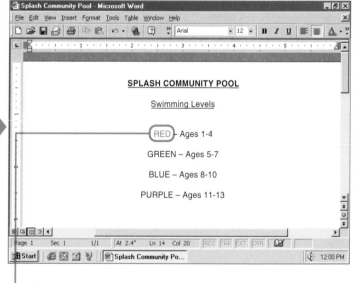

1 Select the text you want to change to a different color. To select text, see page 14.

2 Click ⋮ in this area to select a color.

Note: If ▲⋮ is not displayed, click » on the Formatting toolbar to display all the buttons.

3 Click the color you want to use.

■ The text appears in the color you selected.

■ To deselect text, click outside the selected area.

■ To remove a color from text, repeat steps **1** to **3**, except select **Automatic** in step **3**.

You can highlight text you want to stand out in your document. Highlighting text is useful for marking information you want to review or verify later.

HIGHLIGHT TEXT

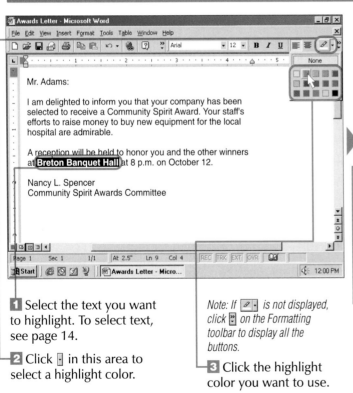

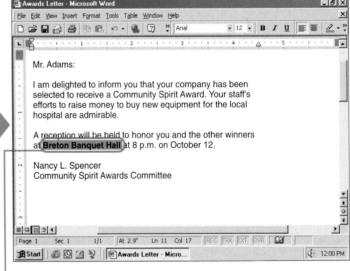

1 Select the text you want to highlight. To select text, see page 14.

2 Click ▯ in this area to select a highlight color.

Note: If ✐ ▾ *is not displayed, click* ⯈ *on the Formatting toolbar to display all the buttons.*

3 Click the highlight color you want to use.

■ The text appears highlighted in the color you selected.

■ To remove a highlight, repeat steps **1** to **3**, except select **None** in step **3**.

You can make text in your document look more attractive by using various fonts, styles, sizes, colors, underlines and special effects.

CHANGE APPEARANCE OF TEXT

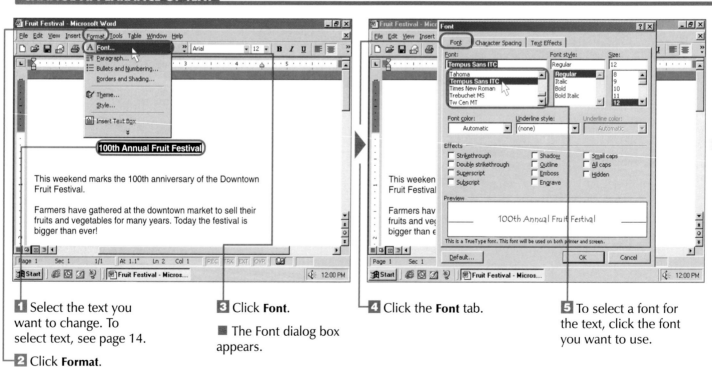

1 Select the text you want to change. To select text, see page 14.

2 Click **Format**.

3 Click **Font**.

■ The Font dialog box appears.

4 Click the **Font** tab.

5 To select a font for the text, click the font you want to use.

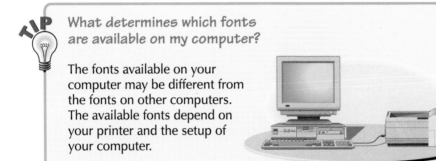

What determines which fonts are available on my computer?

The fonts available on your computer may be different from the fonts on other computers. The available fonts depend on your printer and the setup of your computer.

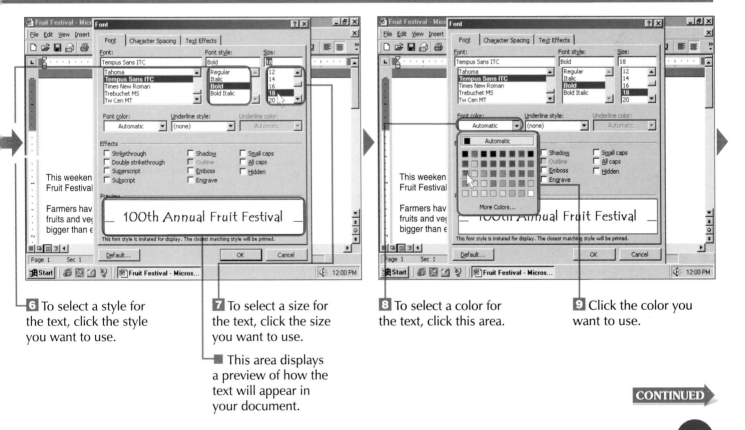

6 To select a style for the text, click the style you want to use.

7 To select a size for the text, click the size you want to use.

■ This area displays a preview of how the text will appear in your document.

8 To select a color for the text, click this area.

9 Click the color you want to use.

CONTINUED

CHANGE APPEARANCE OF TEXT

CHANGE APPEARANCE OF TEXT (CONTINUED)

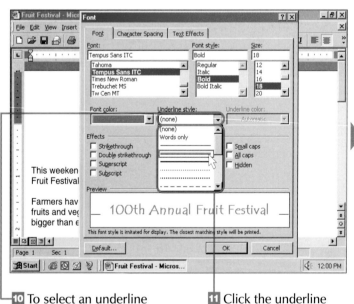

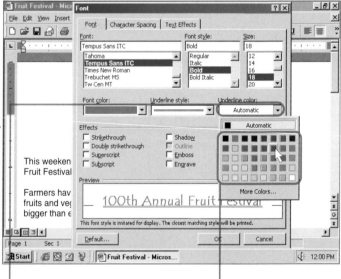

10 To select an underline style for the text, click this area.

11 Click the underline style you want to use.

12 To select a color for the underline, click this area.

Note: You can only select an underline color if you selected an underline style in steps 10 and 11.

13 Click the underline color you want to use.

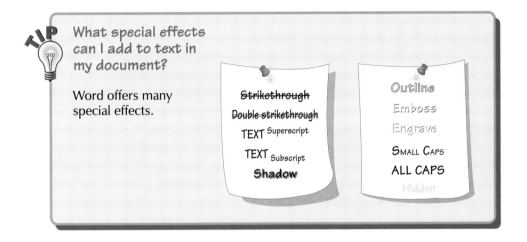

TIP

What special effects can I add to text in my document?

Word offers many special effects.

~~Strikethrough~~

~~Double strikethrough~~

TEXT Superscript

TEXT Subscript

Shadow

Outline

Emboss

Engrave

Sᴍᴀʟʟ Cᴀᴘs

ALL CAPS

Hidden

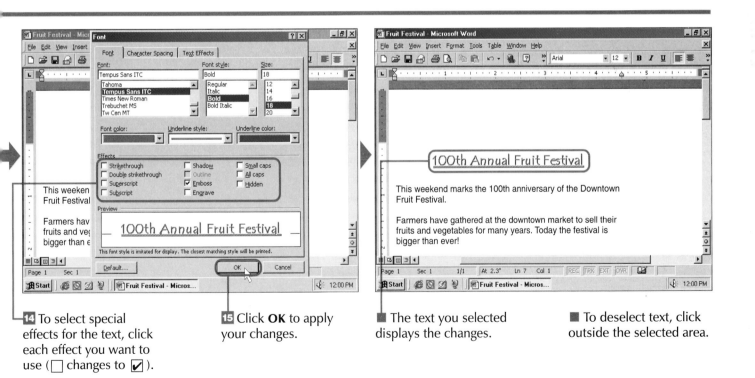

14 To select special effects for the text, click each effect you want to use (☐ changes to ☑).

15 Click **OK** to apply your changes.

■ The text you selected displays the changes.

■ To deselect text, click outside the selected area.

You can change the font that Word uses for all new documents you create. This is useful when you want all future documents to appear in a specific font.

The font that Word uses for all new documents is called the default font.

CHANGE FONT FOR ALL NEW DOCUMENTS

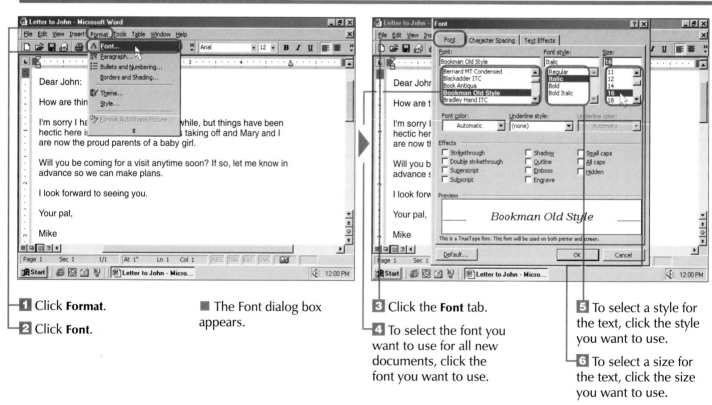

1 Click **Format**.

2 Click **Font**.

■ The Font dialog box appears.

3 Click the **Font** tab.

4 To select the font you want to use for all new documents, click the font you want to use.

5 To select a style for the text, click the style you want to use.

6 To select a size for the text, click the size you want to use.

TIP

Will changing the font for all new documents affect the documents I have already created?

No. Word will not change the font in documents you have already created. To change the font of text in existing documents, see pages 80 to 83.

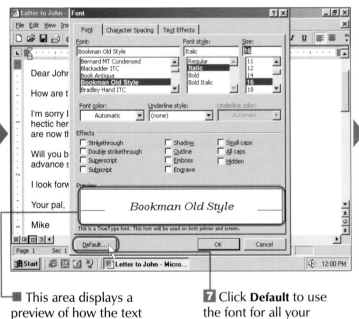

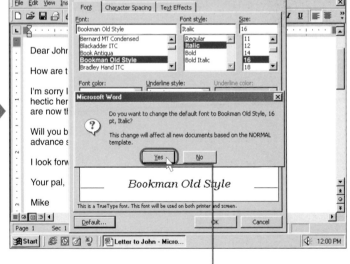

■ This area displays a preview of how the text will appear in your new documents.

7 Click **Default** to use the font for all your new documents.

■ A dialog box appears, asking you to confirm the change.

8 Click **Yes** to confirm the change.

You can make one area of text in your document look exactly like another.

COPY FORMATTING

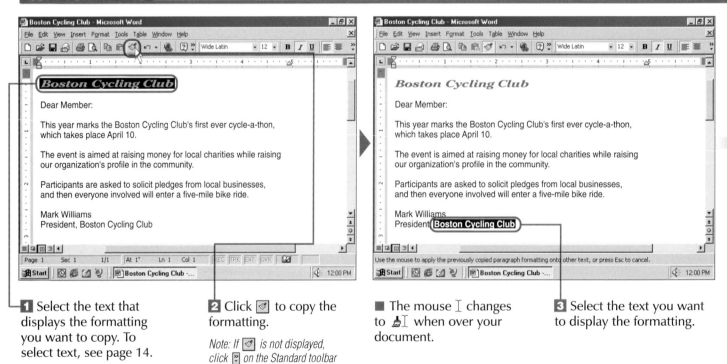

1 Select the text that displays the formatting you want to copy. To select text, see page 14.

2 Click 🖌 to copy the formatting.

Note: If 🖌 is not displayed, click ▸ on the Standard toolbar to display all the buttons.

■ The mouse I changes to 🖌I when over your document.

3 Select the text you want to display the formatting.

Why would I want to copy the formatting of text?

You may want to copy the formatting of text to make all the headings or important words in your document look the same. This will give your document a consistent appearance.

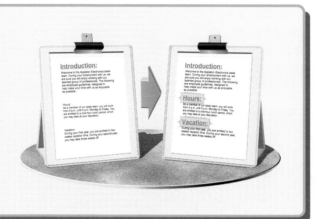

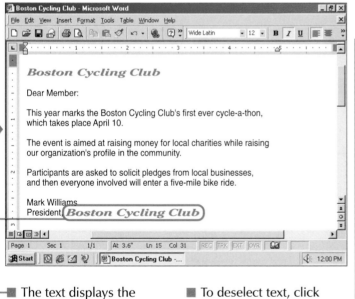

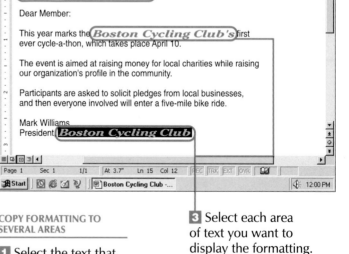

■ The text displays the formatting.

■ To deselect text, click outside the selected area.

COPY FORMATTING TO SEVERAL AREAS

1 Select the text that displays the formatting you want to copy.

2 Double-click ✍ to copy the formatting.

Note: If ✍ is not displayed, click ⣿ on the Standard toolbar to display all the buttons.

3 Select each area of text you want to display the formatting.

4 When you finish copying the formatting, press the Esc key.

CHANGE ALIGNMENT OF TEXT

You can enhance the appearance of your document by aligning text in different ways.

Right Align
Center
Left Align
Justify

CHANGE ALIGNMENT OF TEXT

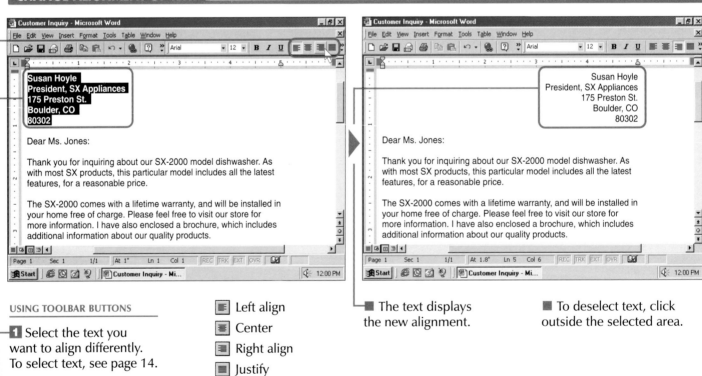

USING TOOLBAR BUTTONS

1 Select the text you want to align differently. To select text, see page 14.

2 Click one of these buttons.

📑 Left align

📑 Center

📑 Right align

📑 Justify

Note: If the button you want is not displayed, click ⸨ on the Formatting toolbar to display all the buttons.

■ The text displays the new alignment.

■ To deselect text, click outside the selected area.

Can I use different alignments within a single line of text?

You can use the Click and Type feature to vary the alignment within a single line of text. For example, you can left align your name and right align the date on the same line.

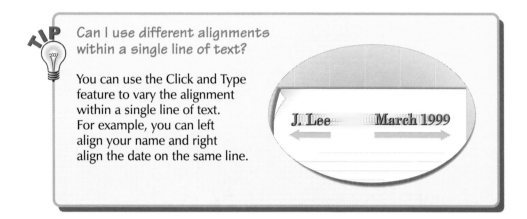

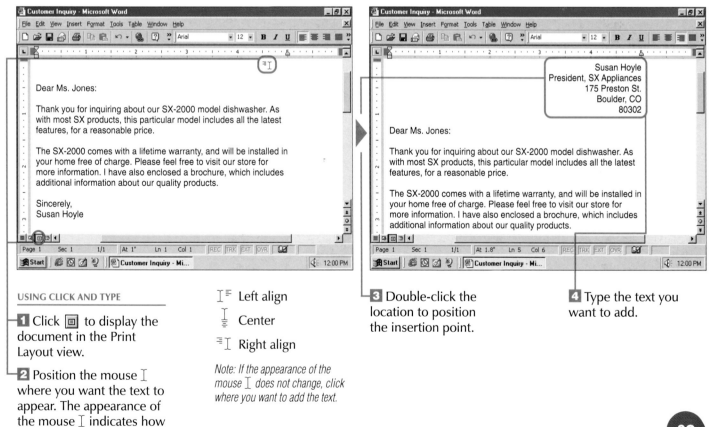

USING CLICK AND TYPE

1 Click 📄 to display the document in the Print Layout view.

2 Position the mouse I where you want the text to appear. The appearance of the mouse I indicates how Word will align the text.

I≡ Left align

I Center

≡I Right align

Note: If the appearance of the mouse I does not change, click where you want to add the text.

3 Double-click the location to position the insertion point.

4 Type the text you want to add.

You can separate items in a list by beginning each item with a bullet or number.

Bullets are useful for items in no particular order, such as items in a shopping list. Numbers are useful for items in a specific order, such as directions in a recipe.

ADD BULLETS OR NUMBERS

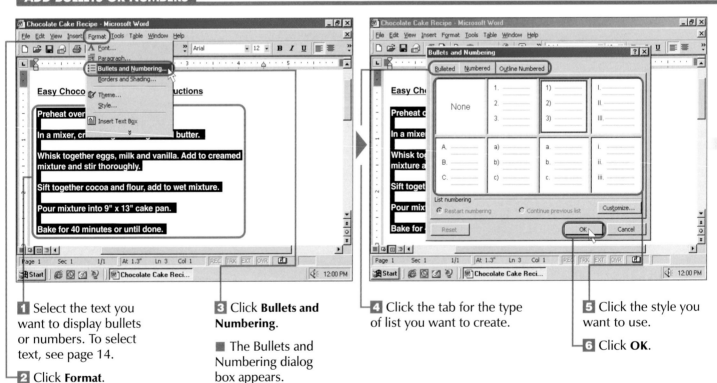

1 Select the text you want to display bullets or numbers. To select text, see page 14.

2 Click **Format**.

3 Click **Bullets and Numbering**.

■ The Bullets and Numbering dialog box appears.

4 Click the tab for the type of list you want to create.

5 Click the style you want to use.

6 Click **OK**.

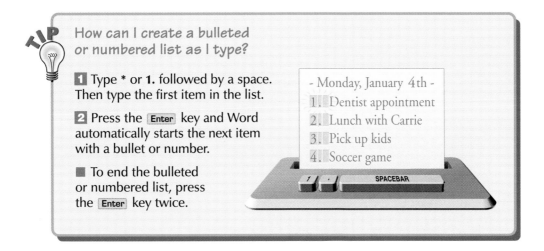

TIP

How can I create a bulleted or numbered list as I type?

1 Type * or **1.** followed by a space. Then type the first item in the list.

2 Press the Enter key and Word automatically starts the next item with a bullet or number.

■ To end the bulleted or numbered list, press the Enter key twice.

- Monday, January 4th -
1. Dentist appointment
2. Lunch with Carrie
3. Pick up kids
4. Soccer game

SPACEBAR

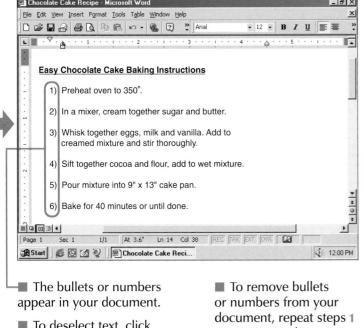

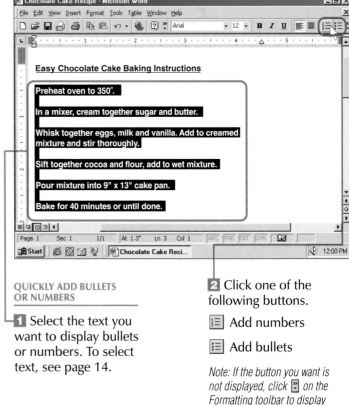

■ The bullets or numbers appear in your document.

■ To deselect text, click outside the selected area.

■ To remove bullets or numbers from your document, repeat steps **1** to **6**, except select **None** in step **5**.

QUICKLY ADD BULLETS OR NUMBERS

1 Select the text you want to display bullets or numbers. To select text, see page 14.

2 Click one of the following buttons.

▦ Add numbers

▤ Add bullets

Note: If the button you want is not displayed, click ⬚ on the Formatting toolbar to display all the buttons.

You can change the amount of space between the lines of text in your document. Changing the line spacing can make your document easier to review and edit.

There is a 10th anniversary High School Reunion on August 6, 7 and 8 at Woodblock High School. We all hope to see you there. Contact Susan Hughes for more information.

Single

There is a 10th anniversary High School Reunion on August 6, 7 and 8 at Woodblock High School. We all hope to see you there. Contact Susan Hughes for more information.

1.5 lines

There is a 10th anniversary High School Reunion on August 6, 7 and 8 at Woodblock High School. We all hope to see you there. Contact Susan Hughes for more information.

Double

CHANGE LINE SPACING

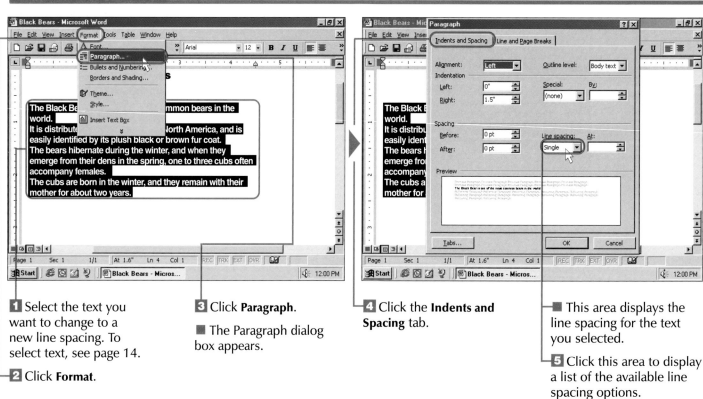

1 Select the text you want to change to a new line spacing. To select text, see page 14.

2 Click **Format**.

3 Click **Paragraph**.

■ The Paragraph dialog box appears.

4 Click the **Indents and Spacing** tab.

■ This area displays the line spacing for the text you selected.

5 Click this area to display a list of the available line spacing options.

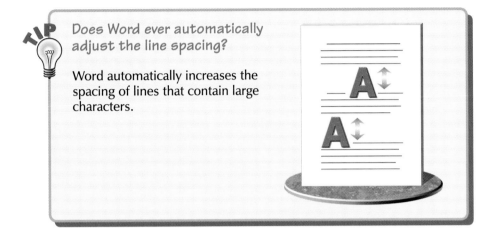

Does Word ever automatically adjust the line spacing?

Word automatically increases the spacing of lines that contain large characters.

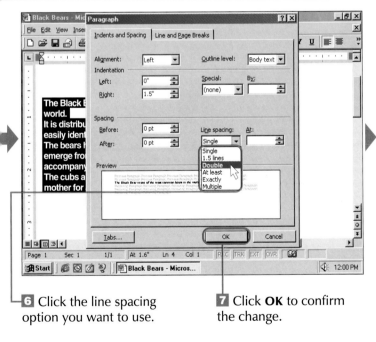

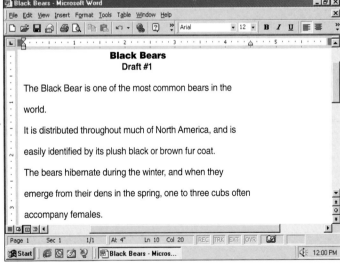

6 Click the line spacing option you want to use.

7 Click **OK** to confirm the change.

■ Word changes the line spacing of the text you selected.

■ To deselect text, click outside the selected area.

INDENT PARAGRAPHS

You can use the Indent feature to make paragraphs in your document stand out.

INDENT PARAGRAPHS

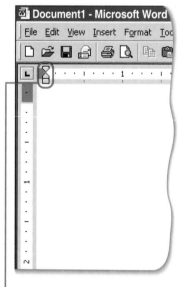

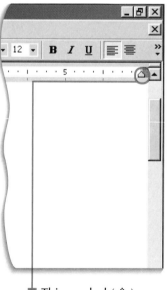

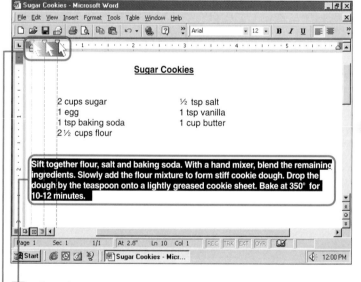

■ These symbols let you indent the left edge of a paragraph.

▽ Indent first line

△ Indent all but first line

☐ Indent all lines

■ This symbol (△) lets you indent the right edge of all the lines in a paragraph.

Note: If the symbols are not displayed, see page 37 to display the ruler.

1 Select the paragraph(s) you want to indent. To select text, see page 14.

2 Drag an indent symbol to a new position.

■ A line shows the new indent position.

TIP

What is a hanging indent?

A hanging indent moves all but the first line of a paragraph to the right. Hanging indents are useful when you are creating a résumé, glossary or bibliography.

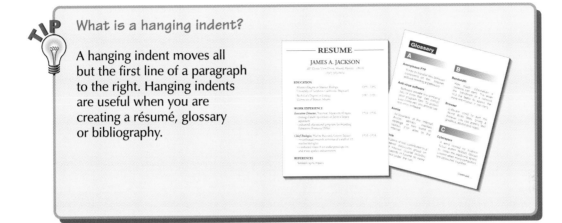

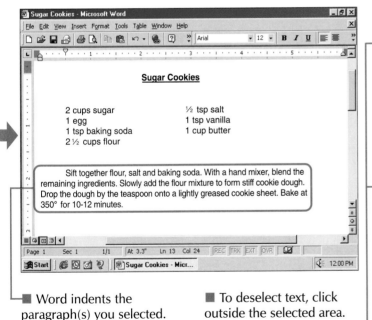

■ Word indents the paragraph(s) you selected.

■ To deselect text, click outside the selected area.

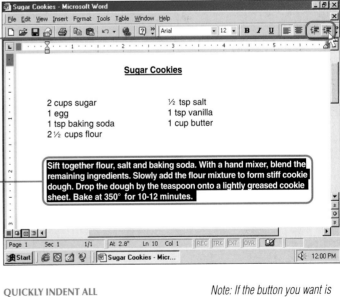

QUICKLY INDENT ALL LINES IN A PARAGRAPH

1 Select the paragraph you want to indent. To select text, see page 14.

2 Click one of the following buttons.

Move paragraph left

Move paragraph right

Note: If the button you want is not displayed, click ⟩⟩ on the Formatting toolbar to display all the buttons.

You can use tabs to line up columns of information in your document. Word offers several types of tabs that you can choose from.

Word automatically places a tab every 0.5 inches across a page.

ADD A TAB

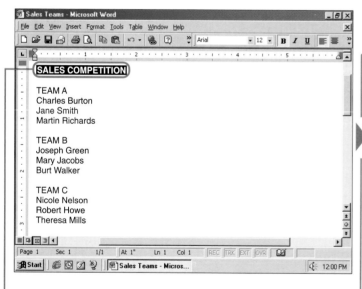

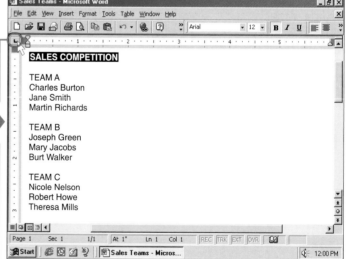

1 Select the text you want to contain the new tab. To select text, see page 14.

■ To add a tab to text you are about to type, click where you want to type the text.

2 Click this area until the type of tab you want to add appears.

Note: If the area is not displayed, see page 37 to display the ruler.

∟	Left tab
⊥	Center tab
⅃	Right tab
⊥	Decimal tab

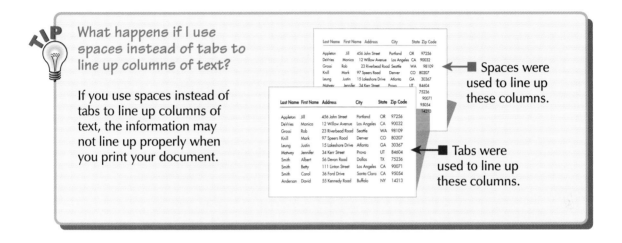

TIP

What happens if I use spaces instead of tabs to line up columns of text?

If you use spaces instead of tabs to line up columns of text, the information may not line up properly when you print your document.

■ Spaces were used to line up these columns.

■ Tabs were used to line up these columns.

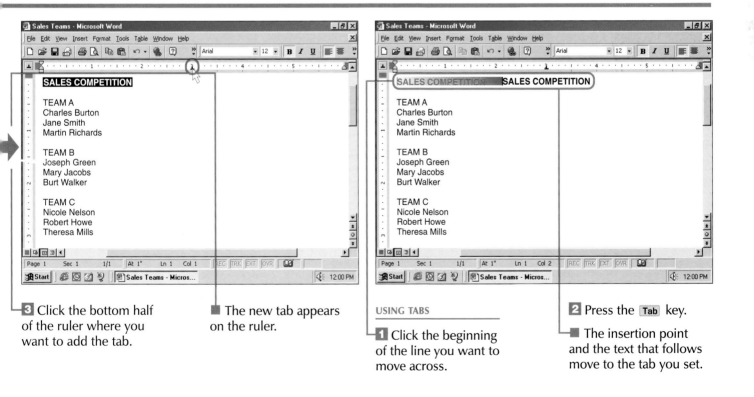

3 Click the bottom half of the ruler where you want to add the tab.

■ The new tab appears on the ruler.

USING TABS

1 Click the beginning of the line you want to move across.

2 Press the Tab key.

■ The insertion point and the text that follows move to the tab you set.

97

CHANGE TAB SETTINGS

You can move a tab to a different position on the ruler.

MOVE A TAB

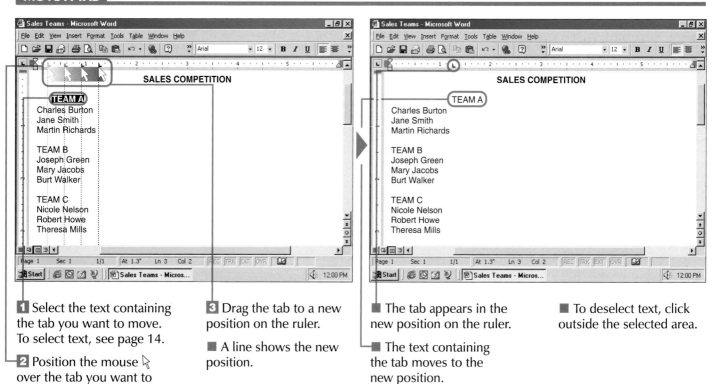

1 Select the text containing the tab you want to move. To select text, see page 14.

2 Position the mouse ▷ over the tab you want to move.

3 Drag the tab to a new position on the ruler.

■ A line shows the new position.

■ The tab appears in the new position on the ruler.

■ The text containing the tab moves to the new position.

■ To deselect text, click outside the selected area.

When you no longer need a tab, you can remove the tab from your document.

REMOVE A TAB

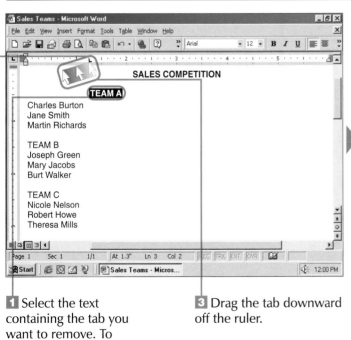

1 Select the text containing the tab you want to remove. To select text, see page 14.

2 Position the mouse over the tab you want to remove.

3 Drag the tab downward off the ruler.

■ The tab disappears from the ruler.

■ To move text back to the left margin, click to the left of the first character. Then press the **+Backspace** key.

You can create a large capital letter at the beginning of a paragraph to enhance the appearance of the paragraph.

Word can only display a drop cap properly in the Print Layout and Web Layout views. For more information on the views, see page 34.

CREATE A DROP CAP

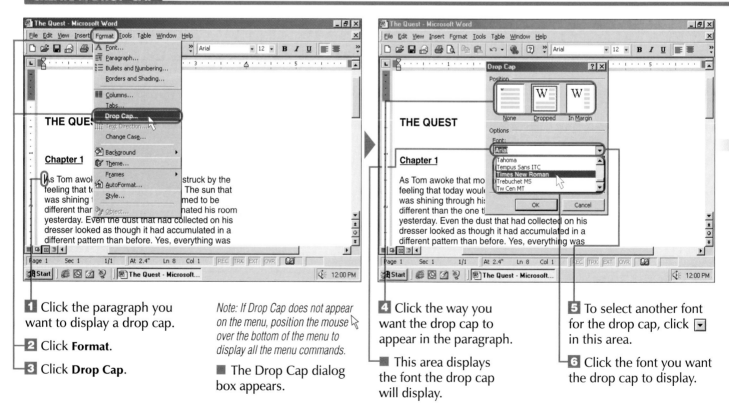

1 Click the paragraph you want to display a drop cap.

2 Click **Format**.

3 Click **Drop Cap**.

Note: If Drop Cap does not appear on the menu, position the mouse over the bottom of the menu to display all the menu commands.

■ The Drop Cap dialog box appears.

4 Click the way you want the drop cap to appear in the paragraph.

■ This area displays the font the drop cap will display.

5 To select another font for the drop cap, click ▾ in this area.

6 Click the font you want the drop cap to display.

Can I create a drop cap using more than one letter?

You can create a drop cap using several letters or an entire word at the beginning of a paragraph. Select the letters or word you want to make a drop cap and then perform steps 2 to 8 below. To select text, see page 14.

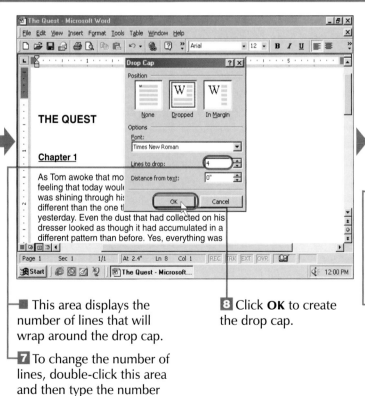

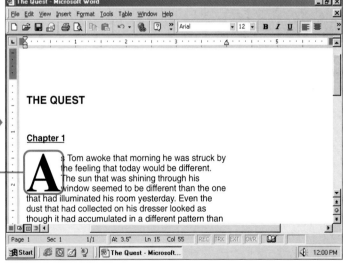

■ This area displays the number of lines that will wrap around the drop cap.

7 To change the number of lines, double-click this area and then type the number of lines.

8 Click **OK** to create the drop cap.

■ The drop cap appears in your document.

■ To deselect the drop cap, click outside the drop cap.

■ To remove a drop cap, repeat steps 1 to 4, selecting **None** in step 4. Then perform step 8.

You can create a style to store formatting you like. You can then use the style to quickly apply the formatting to text in your documents.

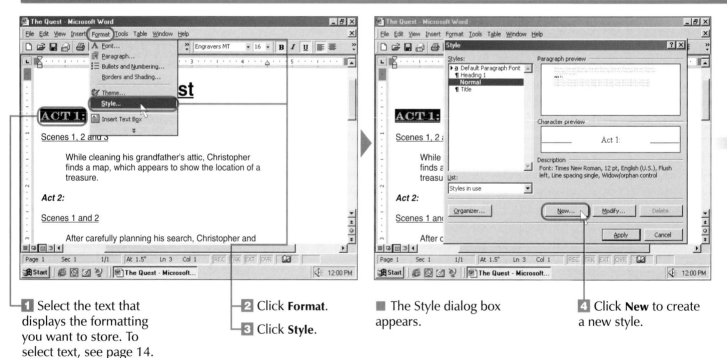

1 Select the text that displays the formatting you want to store. To select text, see page 14.

2 Click **Format**.

3 Click **Style**.

■ The Style dialog box appears.

4 Click **New** to create a new style.

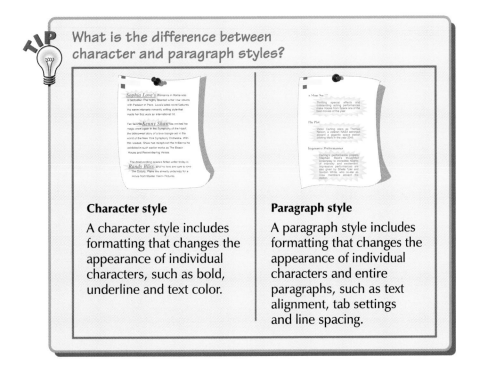

TIP

What is the difference between character and paragraph styles?

Character style

A character style includes formatting that changes the appearance of individual characters, such as bold, underline and text color.

Paragraph style

A paragraph style includes formatting that changes the appearance of individual characters and entire paragraphs, such as text alignment, tab settings and line spacing.

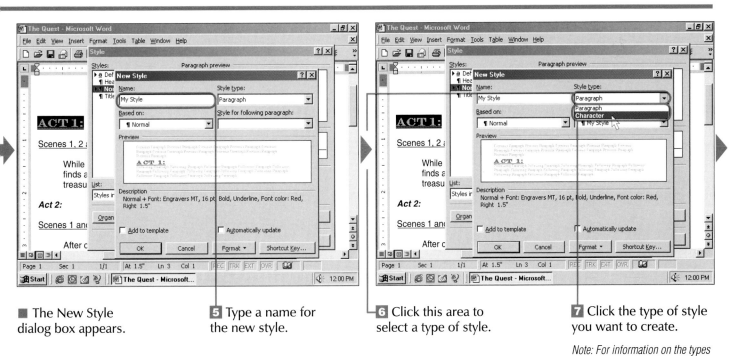

■ The New Style dialog box appears.

5 Type a name for the new style.

6 Click this area to select a type of style.

7 Click the type of style you want to create.

Note: For information on the types of styles, see the top of this page.

CONTINUED

USING STYLES

After you create a style, you can apply the style to text in your document.

CREATE A STYLE (CONTINUED)

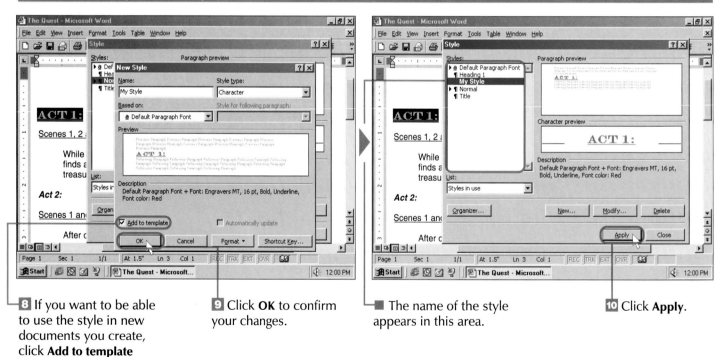

8 If you want to be able to use the style in new documents you create, click **Add to template** (□ changes to ☑).

9 Click **OK** to confirm your changes.

■ The name of the style appears in this area.

10 Click **Apply**.

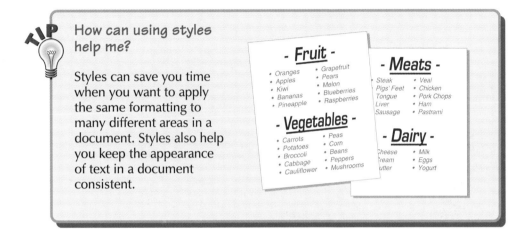

How can using styles help me?

Styles can save you time when you want to apply the same formatting to many different areas in a document. Styles also help you keep the appearance of text in a document consistent.

APPLY A STYLE

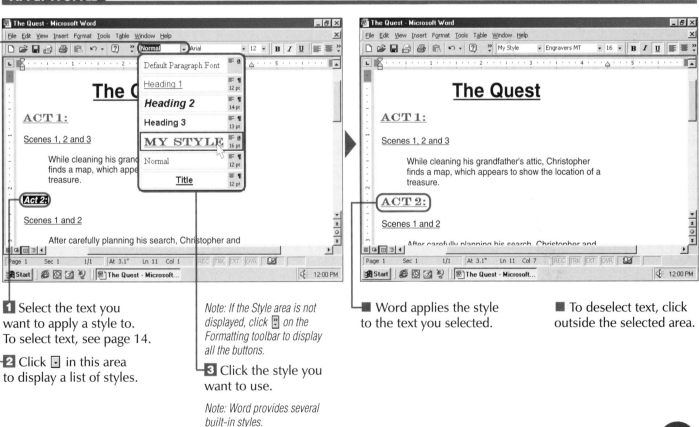

1 Select the text you want to apply a style to. To select text, see page 14.

2 Click ☑ in this area to display a list of styles.

Note: If the Style area is not displayed, click ☒ on the Formatting toolbar to display all the buttons.

3 Click the style you want to use.

Note: Word provides several built-in styles.

■ Word applies the style to the text you selected.

■ To deselect text, click outside the selected area.

You can change a style you created. When you change a style, Word automatically changes all the text you formatted with the style.

CHANGE A STYLE

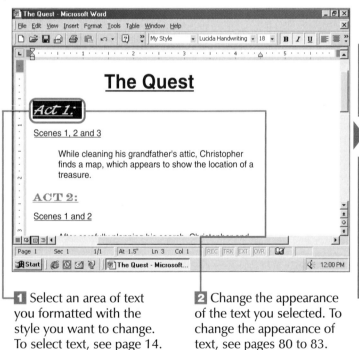

1 Select an area of text you formatted with the style you want to change. To select text, see page 14.

2 Change the appearance of the text you selected. To change the appearance of text, see pages 80 to 83.

3 Click this area and then press the **Enter** key.

Note: If the Style area is not displayed, click ☒ on the Formatting toolbar to display all the buttons.

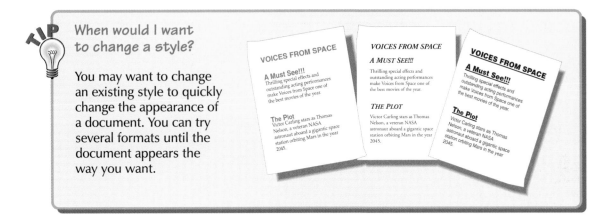

When would I want to change a style?

You may want to change an existing style to quickly change the appearance of a document. You can try several formats until the document appears the way you want.

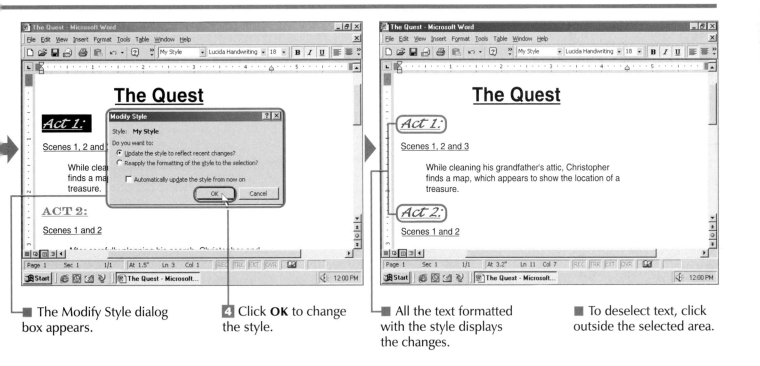

■ The Modify Style dialog box appears.

4 Click **OK** to change the style.

■ All the text formatted with the style displays the changes.

■ To deselect text, click outside the selected area.

The Olympic Flame

One constant that remains from ancient times, is the Olympic flame. It has remained since the beginning.

In ancient times the Olympic games took on a very religious significance. Olympia, the grounds on which the first games were played, was considered sacred.

The ancient Greeks believed very deeply in a relationship between life and death and the connection that existed between religion and burial traditions. For

time the ancient Olympic games were held, the Olympic flame was lit to symbolize the re-birth of the spirit of their dead heroes.

Today, that tradition continues. In 1936, for the first time in modern Olympic history, the sacred Olympic flame was carried to Berlin, Germany where the 11th Olympiad took place. Since that time and to this present day, runners, through a relay, transport the flame, from Greece, every four years to the that is to host the Olympics. runner, carrying the into the stadium at opening Olympic ceremony and lights the Olympic torch which burns throughout the games until it is extinguished during the closing ceremony.

CHAPTER 6

FORMAT PAGES

Are you wondering how to change the appearance of pages in your document? In this chapter you will learn how to add page numbers, change margins, create newspaper columns and more.

You can have Word number the pages in your document.

Word can only display page numbers in the Print Layout view. For more information on the views, see page 34.

If you add, remove or rearrange text in your document, Word will automatically adjust the page numbers for you.

ADD PAGE NUMBERS

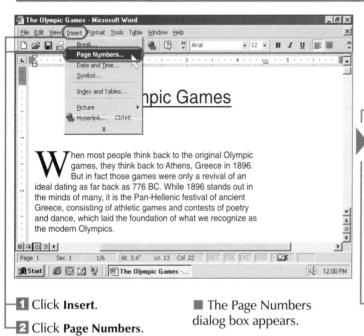

1 Click **Insert**.

2 Click **Page Numbers**.

■ The Page Numbers dialog box appears.

3 Click this area to select a position for the page numbers.

4 Click the position where you want the page numbers to appear.

TIP

How do I remove page numbers from my document?

To remove page numbers, you must delete the page number from the document's header or footer. To delete information from a header or footer, see the top of page 113.

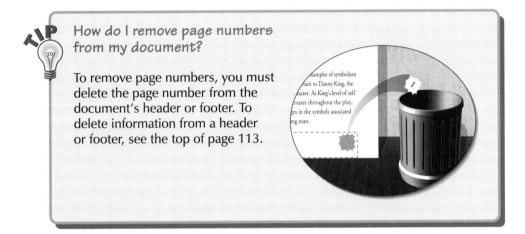

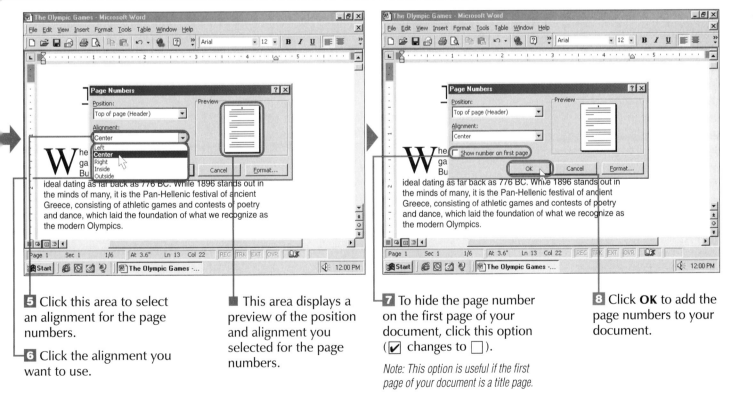

5 Click this area to select an alignment for the page numbers.

6 Click the alignment you want to use.

■ This area displays a preview of the position and alignment you selected for the page numbers.

7 To hide the page number on the first page of your document, click this option (☑ changes to ☐).

Note: This option is useful if the first page of your document is a title page.

8 Click **OK** to add the page numbers to your document.

ADD A HEADER OR FOOTER

You can add a header and footer to every page in your document. A header or footer can display information such as the date, chapter title or your name.

■ A header appears at the top of each page.

■ A footer appears at the bottom of each page.

Word can only display headers and footers in the Print Layout view. For more information on the views, see page 34.

ADD A HEADER OR FOOTER

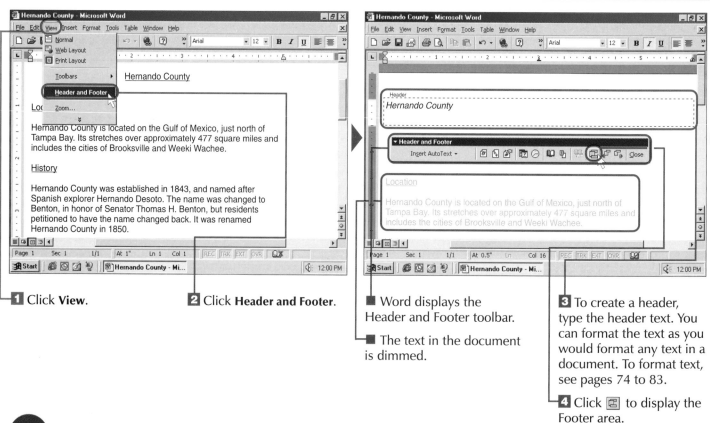

1 Click **View**.

2 Click **Header and Footer**.

■ Word displays the Header and Footer toolbar.

■ The text in the document is dimmed.

3 To create a header, type the header text. You can format the text as you would format any text in a document. To format text, see pages 74 to 83.

4 Click 🔲 to display the Footer area.

How do I delete information from a header or footer?

Perform steps **1** and **2** below to display the headers and footers in your document. Select the text you want to delete from the header or footer and then press the `Delete` key. To select text, see page 14. Deleting information from a header or footer will delete the information from every page in your document.

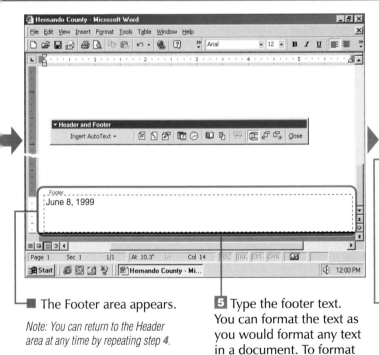

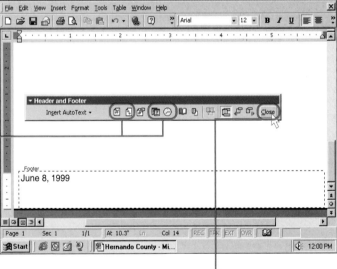

■ The Footer area appears.

Note: You can return to the Header area at any time by repeating step 4.

5 Type the footer text. You can format the text as you would format any text in a document. To format text, see pages 74 to 83.

6 You can click one of the following buttons to quickly insert information into a header or footer.

📑 Page Number

📑 Total Number of Pages

📑 Date

📑 Time

7 When you finish creating the header and footer, click **Close**.

Note: You can repeat steps 1 to 7 to edit the header or footer at any time.

You can add a footnote or endnote to provide additional information about text in your document.

Footnotes and endnotes can provide information such as an explanation, comment or reference.

Word displays footnotes and endnotes as they will appear on a printed page in the Print Layout view. For more information on the views, see page 34.

ADD FOOTNOTES OR ENDNOTES

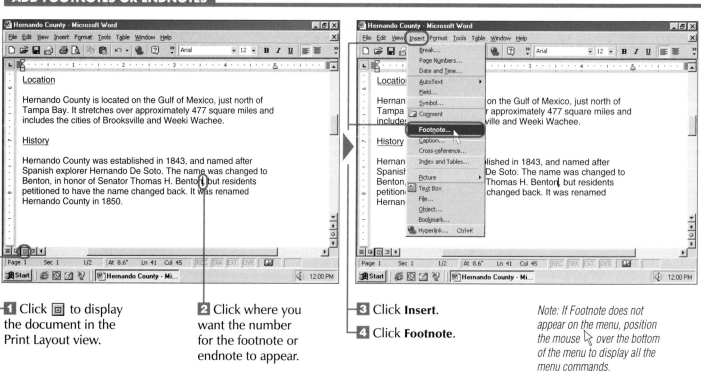

1 Click 🔲 to display the document in the Print Layout view.

2 Click where you want the number for the footnote or endnote to appear.

Note: The number for the footnote or endnote will appear where the insertion point flashes on your screen.

3 Click **Insert**.

4 Click **Footnote**.

Note: If Footnote does not appear on the menu, position the mouse ⍾ over the bottom of the menu to display all the menu commands.

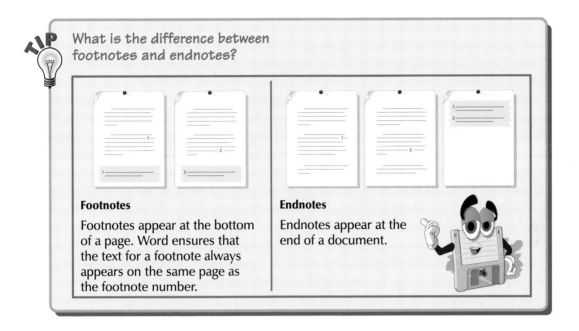

TIP

What is the difference between footnotes and endnotes?

Footnotes

Footnotes appear at the bottom of a page. Word ensures that the text for a footnote always appears on the same page as the footnote number.

Endnotes

Endnotes appear at the end of a document.

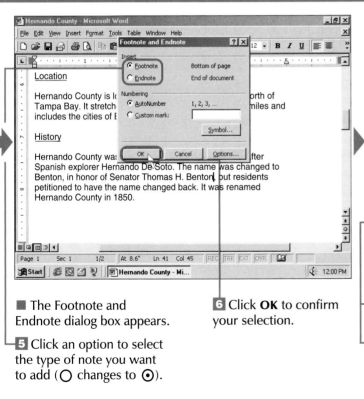

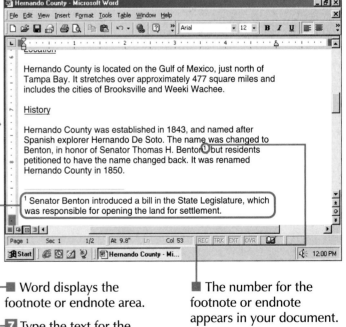

■ The Footnote and Endnote dialog box appears.

5 Click an option to select the type of note you want to add (○ changes to ⊙).

6 Click **OK** to confirm your selection.

■ Word displays the footnote or endnote area.

7 Type the text for the footnote or endnote. You can format the text as you would format any text in a document. To format text, see pages 74 to 83.

■ The number for the footnote or endnote appears in your document.

Note: You may need to scroll through your document to view the number.

ADD FOOTNOTES OR ENDNOTES

You can edit a footnote or endnote you added to a document. You can also delete a footnote or endnote you no longer need.

EDIT A FOOTNOTE OR ENDNOTE

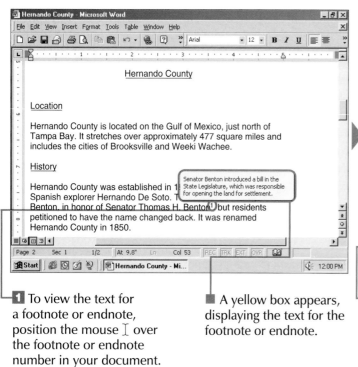

■ **1** To view the text for a footnote or endnote, position the mouse I over the footnote or endnote number in your document.

■ A yellow box appears, displaying the text for the footnote or endnote.

■ **2** To edit the text for a footnote or endnote, click ▤ to display the document in the Print Layout view.

■ **3** Double-click the number for the footnote or endnote you want to edit.

How do I print endnotes on a separate page?

Word automatically prints endnotes after the last line in a document. To print endnotes on a separate page, insert a page break directly above the endnote area. To insert a page break, see page 120.

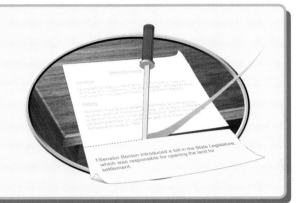

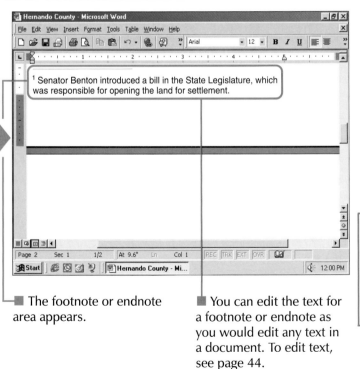

■ The footnote or endnote area appears.

■ You can edit the text for a footnote or endnote as you would edit any text in a document. To edit text, see page 44.

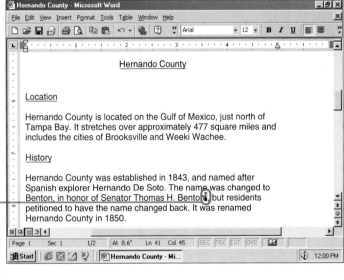

DELETE A FOOTNOTE OR ENDNOTE

1 Select the number for the footnote or endnote you want to delete. To select text, see page 14.

2 Press the Delete key.

■ The footnote or endnote disappears from your document.

■ Word automatically renumbers the remaining footnotes or endnotes in your document.

You can place a border around each page of your document to enhance the appearance of the document.

Word can only display page borders in the Print Layout view. For more information on the views, see page 34.

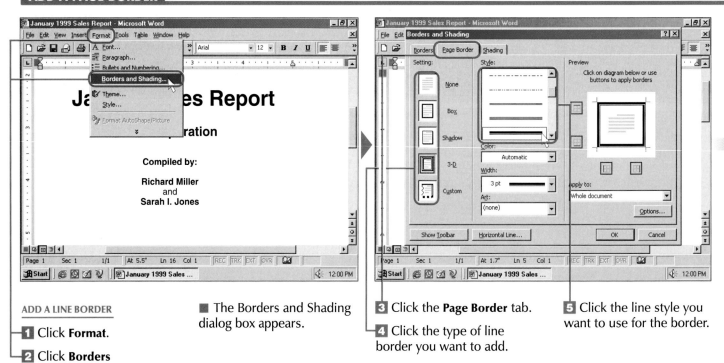

ADD A LINE BORDER

1 Click **Format**.

2 Click **Borders and Shading**.

■ The Borders and Shading dialog box appears.

3 Click the **Page Border** tab.

4 Click the type of line border you want to add.

5 Click the line style you want to use for the border.

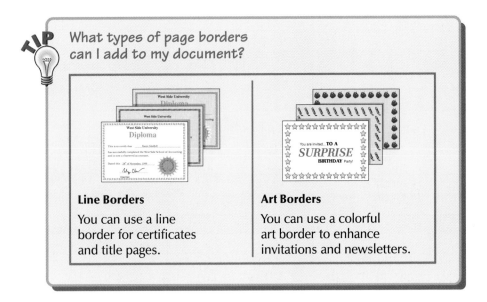

TIP

What types of page borders can I add to my document?

Line Borders

You can use a line border for certificates and title pages.

Art Borders

You can use a colorful art border to enhance invitations and newsletters.

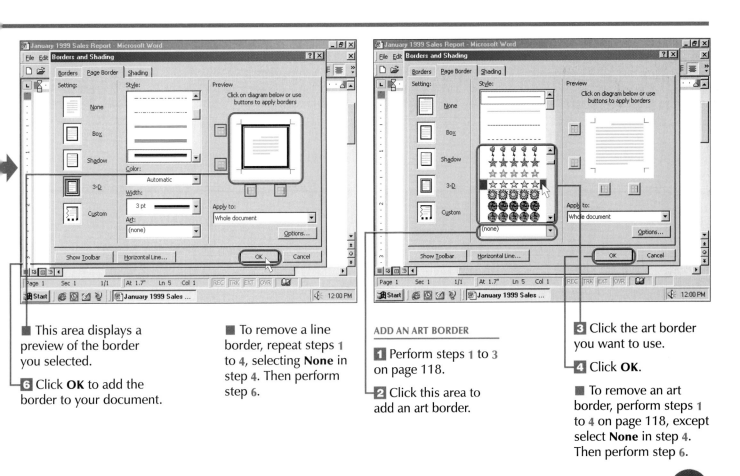

■ This area displays a preview of the border you selected.

6 Click **OK** to add the border to your document.

■ To remove a line border, repeat steps **1** to **4**, selecting **None** in step **4**. Then perform step **6**.

ADD AN ART BORDER

1 Perform steps **1** to **3** on page 118.

2 Click this area to add an art border.

3 Click the art border you want to use.

4 Click **OK**.

■ To remove an art border, perform steps **1** to **4** on page 118, except select **None** in step **4**. Then perform step **6**.

If you want to start a new page at a specific place in your document, you can insert a page break. A page break indicates where one page ends and another begins.

INSERT A PAGE BREAK

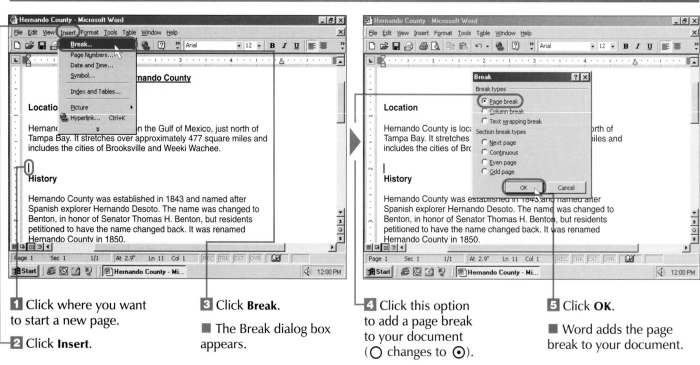

1 Click where you want to start a new page.

2 Click **Insert**.

3 Click **Break**.

■ The Break dialog box appears.

4 Click this option to add a page break to your document (○ changes to ⊙).

5 Click **OK**.

■ Word adds the page break to your document.

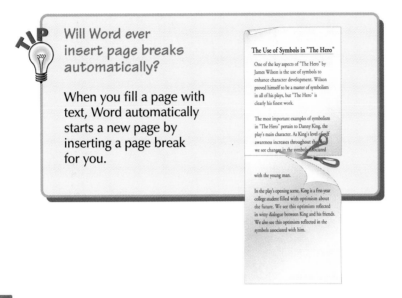

TIP

Will Word ever insert page breaks automatically?

When you fill a page with text, Word automatically starts a new page by inserting a page break for you.

DELETE A PAGE BREAK

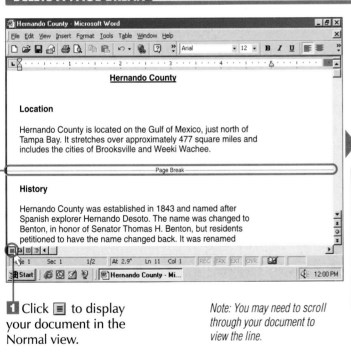

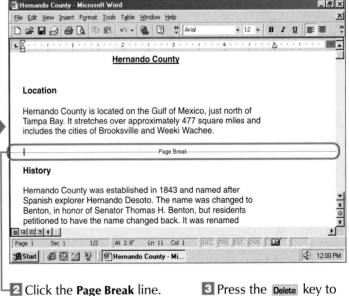

1 Click 📄 to display your document in the Normal view.

■ The **Page Break** line shows where one page ends and another begins. The line will not appear when you print your document.

Note: You may need to scroll through your document to view the line.

2 Click the **Page Break** line.

3 Press the Delete key to remove the page break.

INSERT A SECTION BREAK

You can divide your document into sections so you can format each section separately.

Dividing your document into sections allows you to apply formatting to only part of your document. For example, you may want to add newspaper columns or change the margins for only part of your document.

INSERT A SECTION BREAK

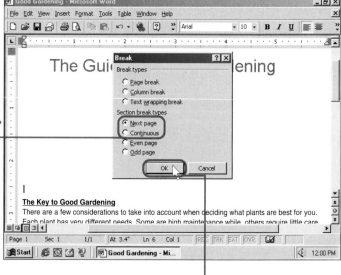

1 Click where you want to start a new section.

2 Click **Insert**.

3 Click **Break**.

■ The Break dialog box appears.

4 Click the type of section break you want to add (○ changes to ⊙).

Next page - Create a new section on a new page

Continuous - Create a new section on the current page

5 Click **OK** to confirm your selection.

■ Word adds the section break to your document.

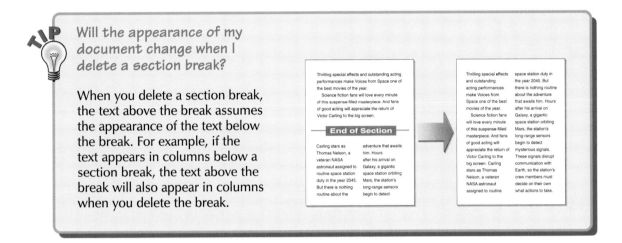

TIP

Will the appearance of my document change when I delete a section break?

When you delete a section break, the text above the break assumes the appearance of the text below the break. For example, if the text appears in columns below a section break, the text above the break will also appear in columns when you delete the break.

DELETE A SECTION BREAK

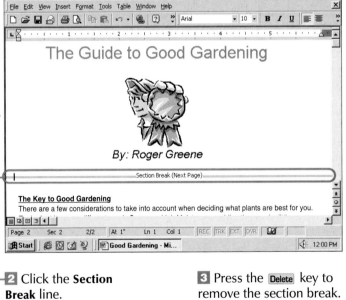

1 Click 📄 to display your document in the Normal view.

■ The **Section Break** line shows where one section ends and another begins. The line will not appear when you print your document.

Note: You may need to scroll through your document to view the line.

2 Click the **Section Break** line.

3 Press the Delete key to remove the section break.

You can vertically center text on each page of your document. This is useful for creating title pages and short memos.

GLOBAL REPORT
Helping the Third World Countries

By: Cathy Best, MBA
University of Washington

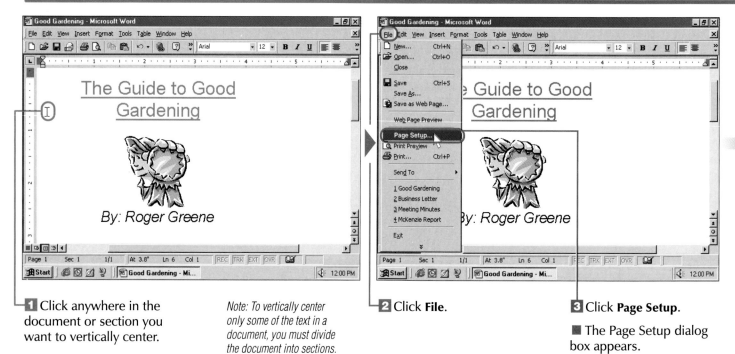

1 Click anywhere in the document or section you want to vertically center.

Note: To vertically center only some of the text in a document, you must divide the document into sections. To divide a document into sections, see page 122.

2 Click **File**.

3 Click **Page Setup**.

■ The Page Setup dialog box appears.

TIP

How can I display the entire page on my screen so I can clearly see how the centered text looks on the page?

You can use the Print Preview feature to display the entire page on your screen. This lets you see how the centered text will appear on a printed page. For information on using Print Preview, see page 134.

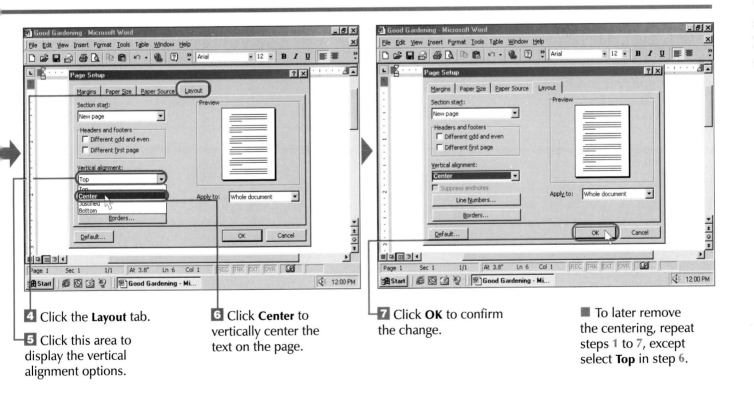

4 Click the **Layout** tab.

5 Click this area to display the vertical alignment options.

6 Click **Center** to vertically center the text on the page.

7 Click **OK** to confirm the change.

■ To later remove the centering, repeat steps 1 to 7, except select **Top** in step 6.

A margin is the amount of space between the text in your document and the edge of your paper. You can change the margins to suit your needs.

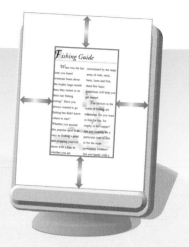

Word automatically sets the top and bottom margins at 1 inch and the left and right margins at 1.25 inches.

Changing margins lets you accommodate letterhead and other specialty paper.

CHANGE MARGINS

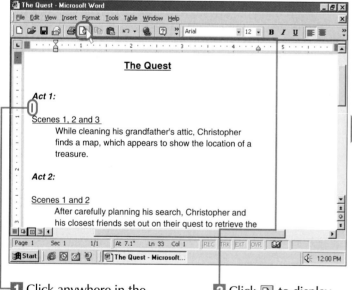

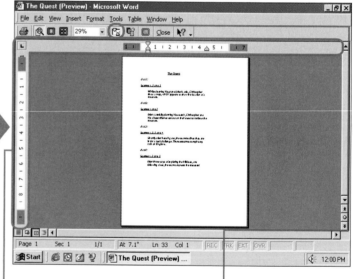

1 Click anywhere in the document or section where you want to change the margins.

Note: To change the margins for only part of a document, you must divide the document into sections. To divide a document into sections, see page 122.

2 Click 🔍 to display your document in the Print Preview window.

Note: If 🔍 is not displayed, click ➤ on the Standard toolbar to display all the buttons.

■ The document appears in the Print Preview window.

Note: For more information on the Print Preview feature, see page 134.

■ This area displays the ruler.

■ If the ruler is not displayed, click 🔲.

TIP

How can I quickly change the left and right margins for only part of my document?

You can change the indentation of paragraphs to quickly change the left and right margins for only part of your document. To indent paragraphs, see page 94.

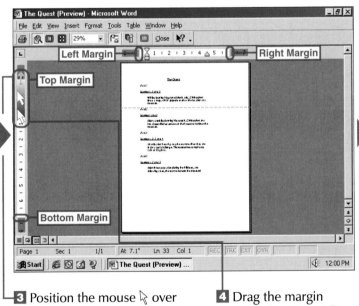

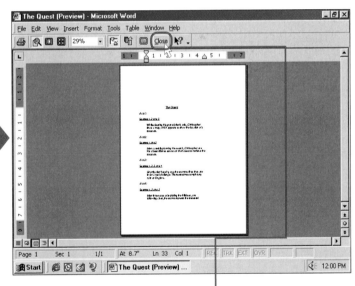

3 Position the mouse ⌖ over a margin you want to change (⌖ changes to ↕ or ↔).

4 Drag the margin to a new location. A line shows the new location.

Note: To view the exact measurement of a margin, press and hold down the **Alt** *key as you drag the margin.*

■ The margin moves to the new location.

5 Repeat steps **3** and **4** for each margin you want to change.

6 When you finish changing the margins, click **Close** to close the Print Preview window.

You can change the orientation of pages in your document. The page orientation determines the direction that information prints on a page.

Portrait

The Olympic Flame

Landscape

The Olympic Flame

CHANGE PAGE ORIENTATION

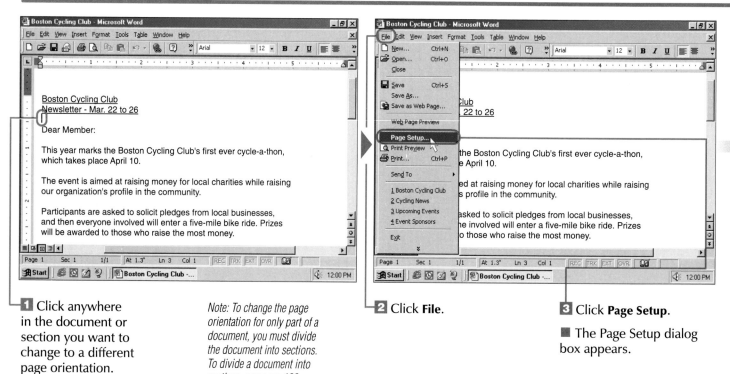

1 Click anywhere in the document or section you want to change to a different page orientation.

Note: To change the page orientation for only part of a document, you must divide the document into sections. To divide a document into sections, see page 122.

2 Click **File**.

3 Click **Page Setup**.

■ The Page Setup dialog box appears.

Which page orientation should I use?

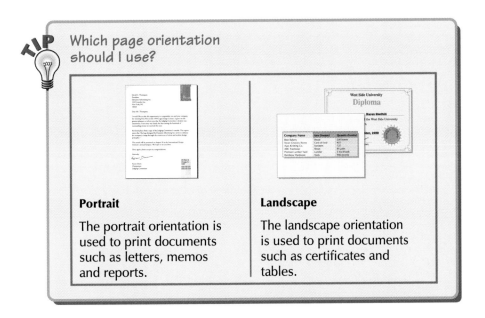

Portrait

The portrait orientation is used to print documents such as letters, memos and reports.

Landscape

The landscape orientation is used to print documents such as certificates and tables.

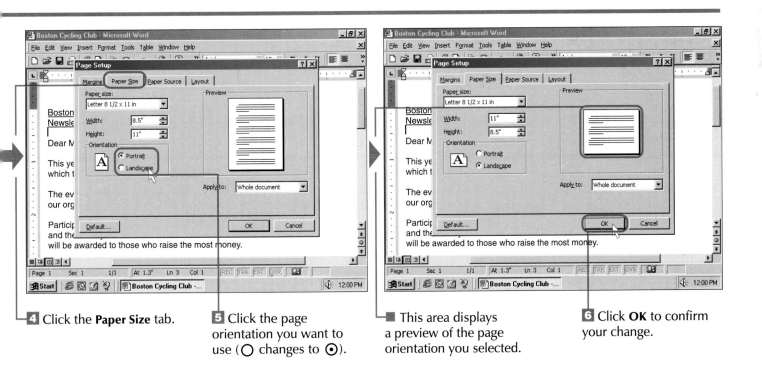

4 Click the **Paper Size** tab.

5 Click the page orientation you want to use (○ changes to ⊙).

■ This area displays a preview of the page orientation you selected.

6 Click **OK** to confirm your change.

You can display text in columns like those found in a newspaper. This is useful for creating documents such as newsletters and brochures.

CREATE NEWSPAPER COLUMNS

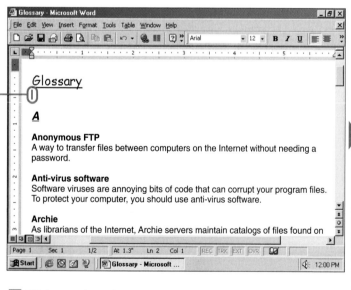

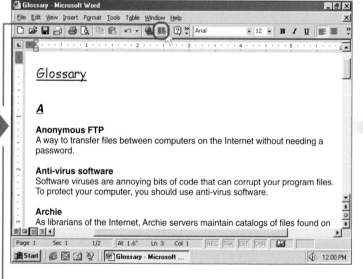

1 Click anywhere in the document or section you want to display in newspaper columns.

Note: To create newspaper columns for only part of a document, you must divide the document into sections. To divide a document into sections, see page 122.

2 Click ▦ to create newspaper columns.

Note: If ▦ is not displayed, click ⟫ on the Standard toolbar to display all the buttons.

TIP

Why didn't my text appear in newspaper columns?

Word can only display newspaper columns side-by-side in the Print Layout view. For more information on the views, see page 34.

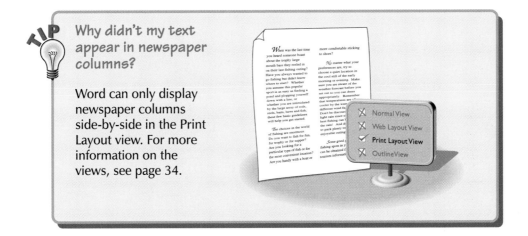

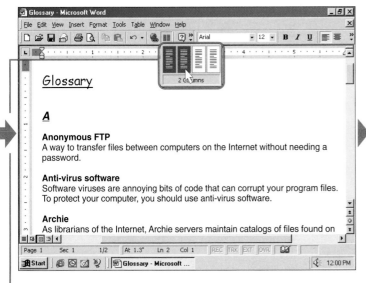

3 Drag the mouse ⌖ until you highlight the number of columns you want to create.

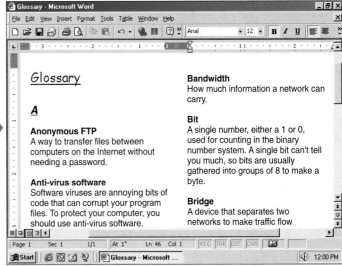

■ The text in the document appears in newspaper columns.

■ To remove newspaper columns, repeat steps **1** to **3**, selecting one column in step **3**.

CHAPTER 7

PRINT DOCUMENTS

Would you like to produce a paper copy of a document? In this chapter you will learn how to print your documents, envelopes and labels.

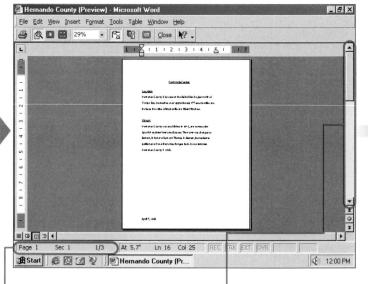

You can use the Print Preview feature to see how your document will look when printed. This lets you confirm that the document will print the way you want.

PREVIEW A DOCUMENT

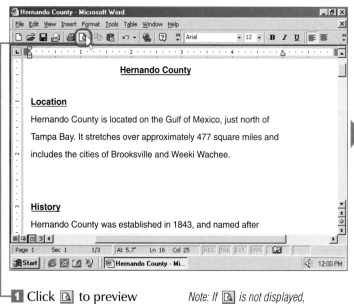

1 Click 🔍 to preview your document.

Note: If 🔍 is not displayed, click ☒ on the Standard toolbar to display all the buttons.

■ The Print Preview window appears, displaying a page from your document.

■ This area indicates which page is displayed and the total number of pages in your document.

■ If your document contains more than one page, you can use the scroll bar to view the other pages.

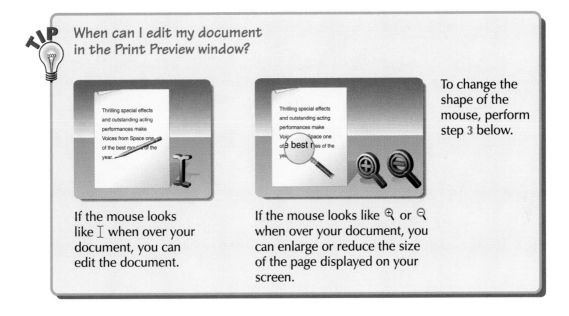

When can I edit my document in the Print Preview window?

If the mouse looks like I when over your document, you can edit the document.

If the mouse looks like ⊕ or ⊖ when over your document, you can enlarge or reduce the size of the page displayed on your screen.

To change the shape of the mouse, perform step 3 below.

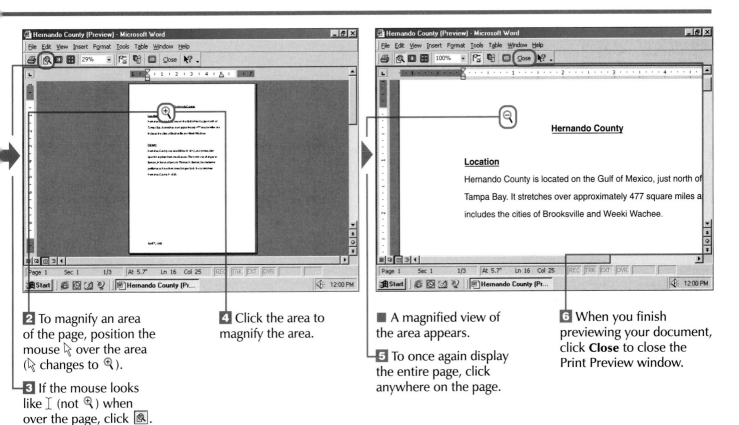

2 To magnify an area of the page, position the mouse ⌀ over the area (⌀ changes to ⊕).

3 If the mouse looks like I (not ⊕) when over the page, click 🔍.

4 Click the area to magnify the area.

■ A magnified view of the area appears.

5 To once again display the entire page, click anywhere on the page.

6 When you finish previewing your document, click **Close** to close the Print Preview window.

135

You can produce a paper copy of the document displayed on your screen.

Before printing your document, make sure the printer is turned on and contains an adequate supply of paper.

PRINT A DOCUMENT

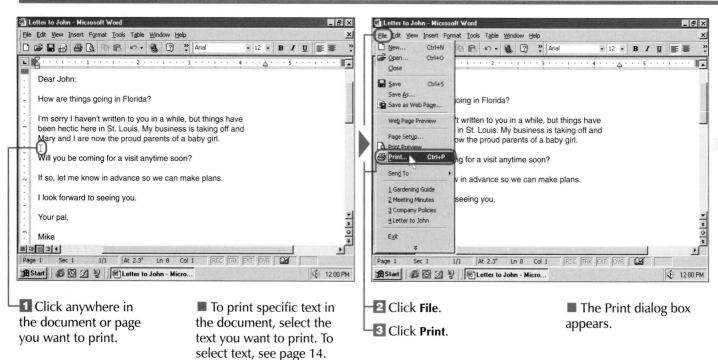

1 Click anywhere in the document or page you want to print.

■ To print specific text in the document, select the text you want to print. To select text, see page 14.

2 Click **File**.

3 Click **Print**.

■ The Print dialog box appears.

TIP

Which print option should I use?

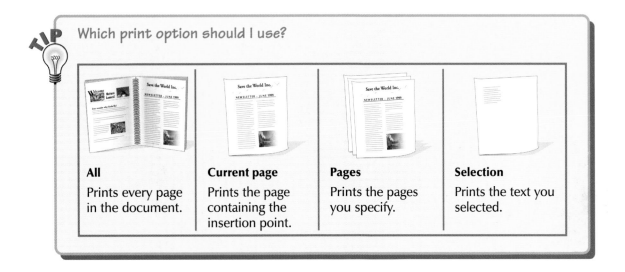

All
Prints every page in the document.

Current page
Prints the page containing the insertion point.

Pages
Prints the pages you specify.

Selection
Prints the text you selected.

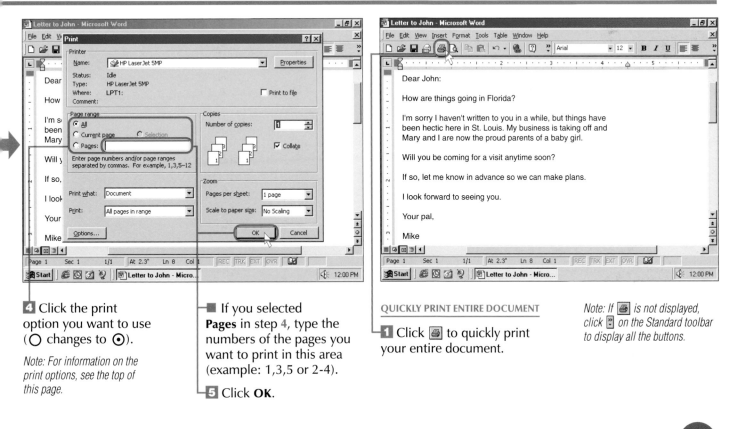

4 Click the print option you want to use (○ changes to ⊙).

Note: For information on the print options, see the top of this page.

■ If you selected **Pages** in step **4**, type the numbers of the pages you want to print in this area (example: 1,3,5 or 2-4).

5 Click **OK**.

QUICKLY PRINT ENTIRE DOCUMENT

1 Click 🖨 to quickly print your entire document.

Note: If 🖨 is not displayed, click ⯈ on the Standard toolbar to display all the buttons.

You can print an address on an envelope.

Before you begin, make sure your printer can print envelopes. You can consult the manual that came with your printer to determine if your printer can print envelopes.

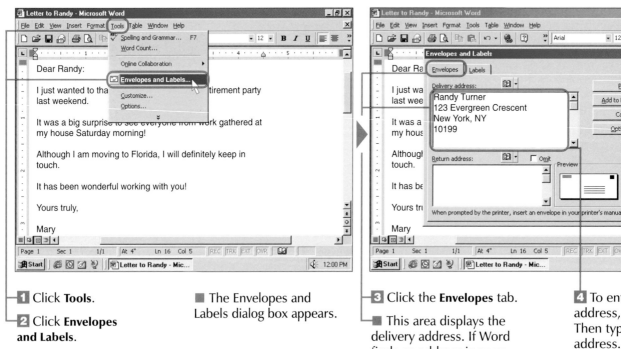

1 Click **Tools**.

2 Click **Envelopes and Labels**.

■ The Envelopes and Labels dialog box appears.

3 Click the **Envelopes** tab.

■ This area displays the delivery address. If Word finds an address in your document, Word will enter the address for you.

4 To enter a delivery address, click this area. Then type the delivery address.

Note: To remove any existing text before typing an address, drag the mouse I over the text until you highlight the text. Then press the Delete *key.*

138

Can I make an envelope part of my document?

Yes. To make an envelope part of your document, perform steps **1** to **7** below, except select **Add to Document** in step **6**. The envelope appears before the first page in your document. You can edit, format, save and print the envelope as part of your document.

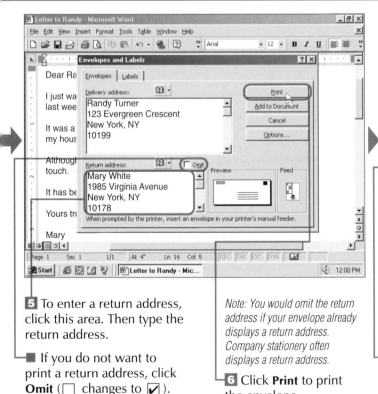

5 To enter a return address, click this area. Then type the return address.

■ If you do not want to print a return address, click **Omit** (☐ changes to ☑).

Note: You would omit the return address if your envelope already displays a return address. Company stationery often displays a return address.

6 Click **Print** to print the envelope.

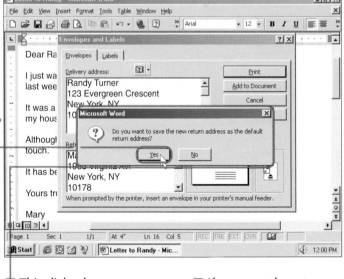

■ This dialog box appears if you entered a return address.

7 To save the return address, click **Yes**.

■ If you save the return address, the address will appear as the return address every time you print an envelope. This saves you from constantly having to retype the address.

You can use Word to print labels. Labels are useful for addressing envelopes, creating name tags and labeling file folders.

PRINT LABELS

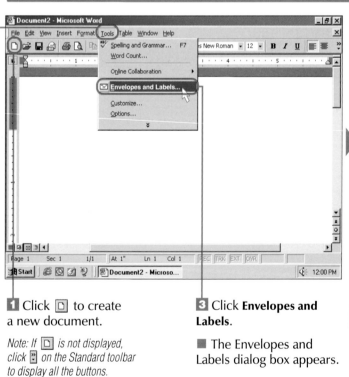

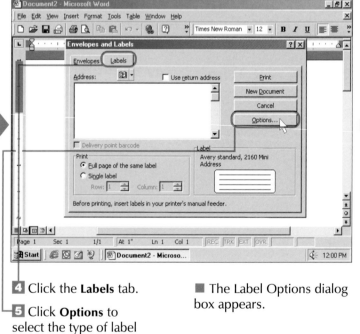

1 Click ▢ to create a new document.

Note: If ▢ is not displayed, click ⊠ on the Standard toolbar to display all the buttons.

2 Click **Tools**.

3 Click **Envelopes and Labels**.

■ The Envelopes and Labels dialog box appears.

4 Click the **Labels** tab.

5 Click **Options** to select the type of label you will use.

■ The Label Options dialog box appears.

TIP

Which label product and type should I choose?

You can check your label packaging to determine which label product and type you should choose.

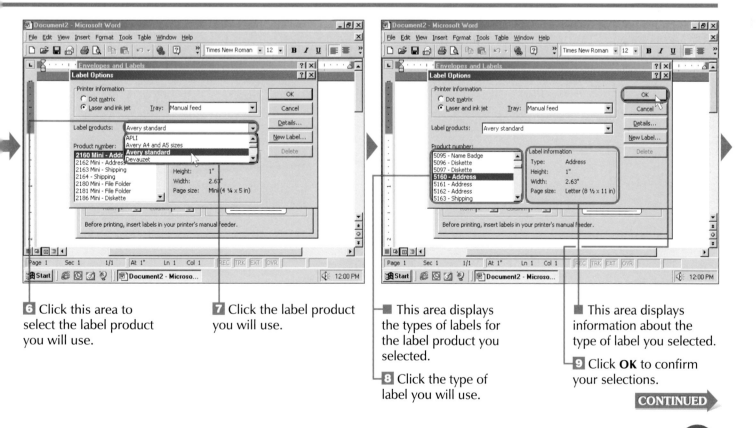

6 Click this area to select the label product you will use.

7 Click the label product you will use.

■ This area displays the types of labels for the label product you selected.

8 Click the type of label you will use.

■ This area displays information about the type of label you selected.

9 Click **OK** to confirm your selections.

CONTINUED

After you create the labels, you can enter the information you want to appear on each label.

Ms. Spencer
6757 Main Street
Las Vegas, NV 89199

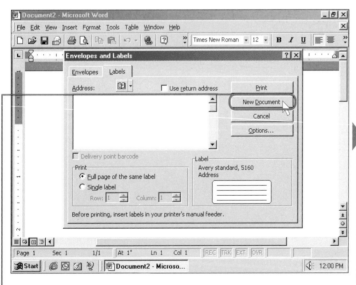

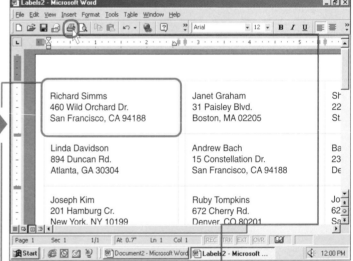

Richard Simms
460 Wild Orchard Dr.
San Francisco, CA 94188

Janet Graham
31 Paisley Blvd.
Boston, MA 02205

Linda Davidson
894 Duncan Rd.
Atlanta, GA 30304

Andrew Bach
15 Constellation Dr.
San Francisco, CA 94188

Joseph Kim
201 Hamburg Cr.
New York, NY 10199

Ruby Tompkins
672 Cherry Rd.
Denver, CO 80201

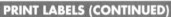

■10 Click **New Document** to add the labels to a new document.

■ The labels appear in a new document.

■11 Click a label where you want to enter text and then type the text. Repeat this step for each label.

Note: You can format the text on the labels as you would format any text in a document. To format text, see pages 74 to 83.

■12 Click 🖨 to print the labels.

Note: If 🖨 is not displayed, click 💲 on the Standard toolbar to display all the buttons.

TIP

Can I quickly create a label for each person on my mailing list?

You can use the Mail Merge feature included with Word to quickly create a label for each person on your mailing list. For information on using the Mail Merge feature to create labels, see page 202.

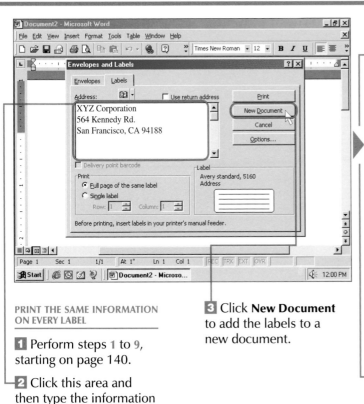

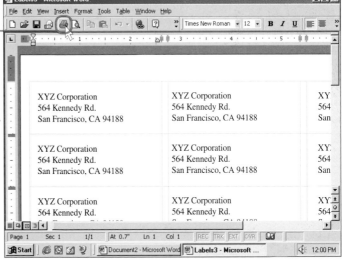

PRINT THE SAME INFORMATION ON EVERY LABEL

1 Perform steps **1** to **9**, starting on page 140.

2 Click this area and then type the information you want to appear on every label.

3 Click **New Document** to add the labels to a new document.

■ The labels appear in a new document. Each label displays the same information.

4 Click 🖨 to print the labels.

Note: If 🖨 is not displayed, click ⬛ on the Standard toolbar to display all the buttons.

143

CHAPTER 8

WORK WITH MULTIPLE DOCUMENTS

Are you interested in working with more than one document at a time? In this chapter you will learn how to switch between documents, move or copy text between documents and more.

You can create a new document to start writing a letter, memo or report.

Think of each document as a separate piece of paper. Creating a new document is like placing a new piece of paper on your screen.

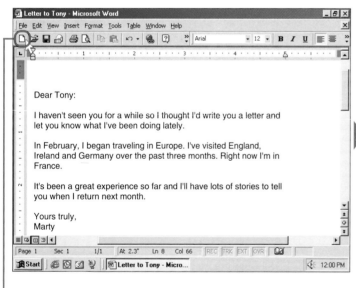

1 Click ⬜ to create a new document.

Note: If ⬜ is not displayed, click ≫ on the Standard toolbar to display all the buttons.

■ A new document appears. The previous document is now hidden behind the new document.

■ A button for the new document appears on the taskbar.

SWITCH BETWEEN DOCUMENTS

Word lets you have many documents open at once. You can easily switch from one open document to another.

SWITCH BETWEEN DOCUMENTS

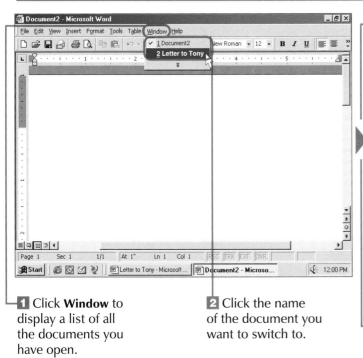

1 Click **Window** to display a list of all the documents you have open.

2 Click the name of the document you want to switch to.

■ The document appears.

■ Word displays the name of the current document at the top of your screen.

■ The taskbar displays a button for each open document. You can also switch to a document by clicking its button on the taskbar.

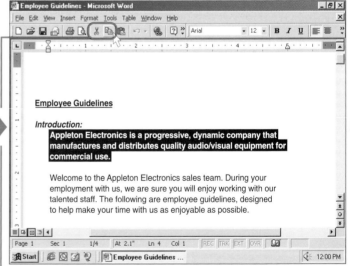

You can move or copy text from one document to another. This will save you time when you want to use text from another document.

MOVE OR COPY TEXT BETWEEN DOCUMENTS

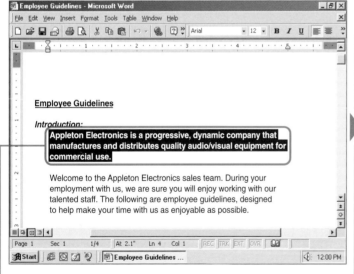

1 Select the text you want to move or copy to another document. To select text, see page 14.

2 Click one of the following buttons.

⬚ Move text

⬚ Copy text

Note: If the button you want is not displayed, click ⬚ on the Standard toolbar to display all the buttons.

Note: The Clipboard toolbar may appear when you move or copy text. To use the Clipboard toolbar, see page 51.

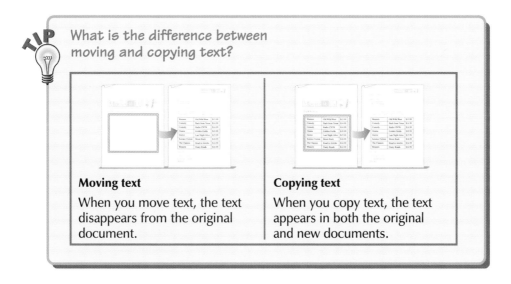

TIP

What is the difference between moving and copying text?

Moving text

When you move text, the text disappears from the original document.

Copying text

When you copy text, the text appears in both the original and new documents.

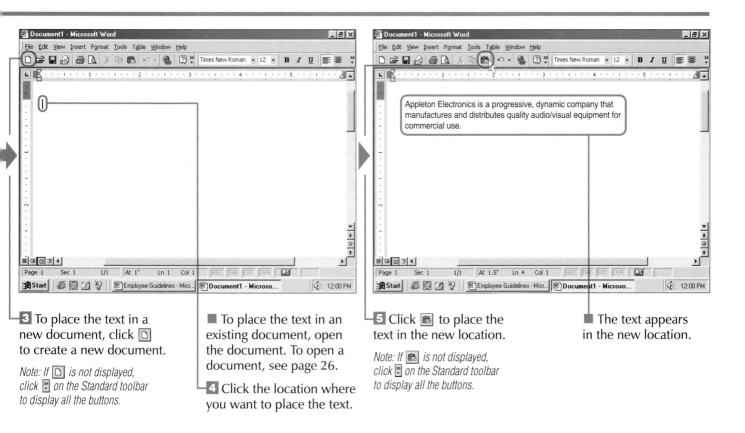

3 To place the text in a new document, click ![new] to create a new document.

Note: If ![new] is not displayed, click ![more] on the Standard toolbar to display all the buttons.

■ To place the text in an existing document, open the document. To open a document, see page 26.

4 Click the location where you want to place the text.

5 Click ![paste] to place the text in the new location.

Note: If ![paste] is not displayed, click ![more] on the Standard toolbar to display all the buttons.

■ The text appears in the new location.

USING TEMPLATES AND WIZARDS

Template

A template is a document that provides areas for you to fill in your personalized information.

Wizard

A wizard asks you a series of questions and then uses your answers to create a document.

You can use templates and wizards to save time when creating common types of documents, such as letters, memos and reports.

USING TEMPLATES AND WIZARDS

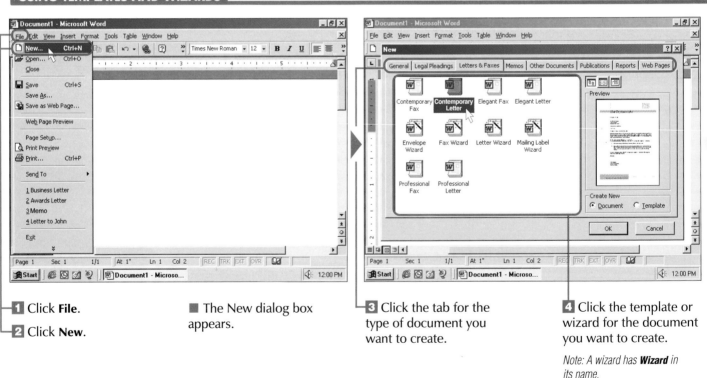

1 Click **File**.

2 Click **New**.

■ The New dialog box appears.

3 Click the tab for the type of document you want to create.

4 Click the template or wizard for the document you want to create.

*Note: A wizard has **Wizard** in its name.*

150

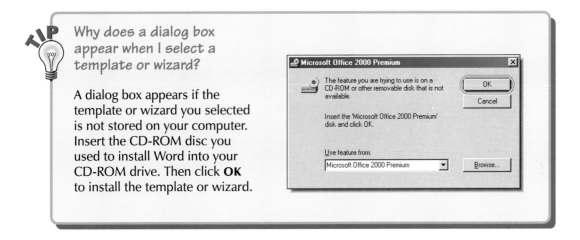

Why does a dialog box appear when I select a template or wizard?

A dialog box appears if the template or wizard you selected is not stored on your computer. Insert the CD-ROM disc you used to install Word into your CD-ROM drive. Then click **OK** to install the template or wizard.

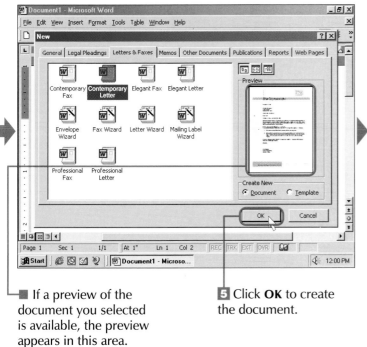

■ If a preview of the document you selected is available, the preview appears in this area.

5 Click **OK** to create the document.

■ The document appears on your screen.

Note: If you selected a wizard in step 4, Word will ask you a series of questions before creating the document.

6 Type your personalized information in the appropriate areas to complete the document.

CHAPTER 9

WORK WITH TABLES

Do you want to learn how to display information in a table? This chapter teaches you how to create and work with tables in your document.

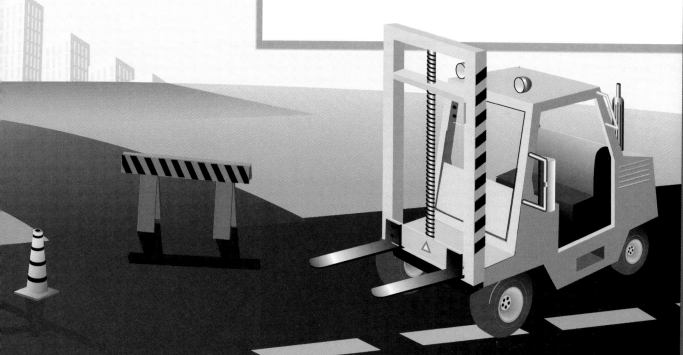

You can create a table to neatly display columns of information in your document.

CREATE A TABLE

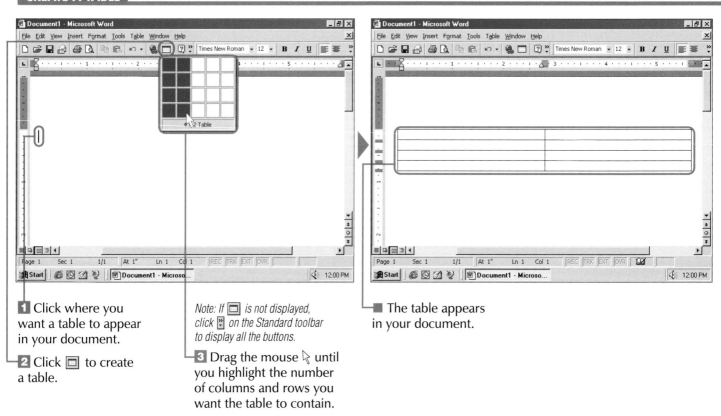

1 Click where you want a table to appear in your document.

2 Click ▦ to create a table.

Note: If ▦ is not displayed, click ☒ on the Standard toolbar to display all the buttons.

3 Drag the mouse ⬚ until you highlight the number of columns and rows you want the table to contain.

■ The table appears in your document.

What are the parts of a table?

A table consists of columns, rows and cells.

■ A column is a vertical line of boxes.

■ A row is a horizontal line of boxes.

■ A cell is one box.

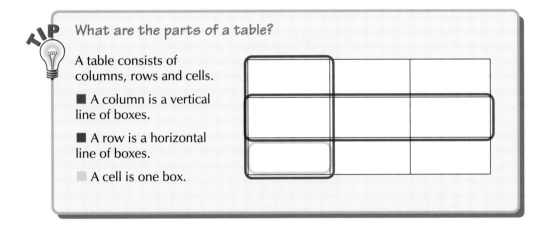

DELETE A TABLE

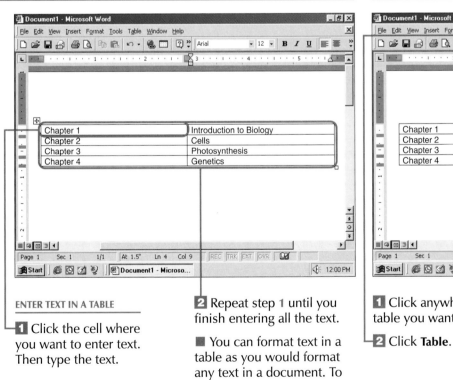

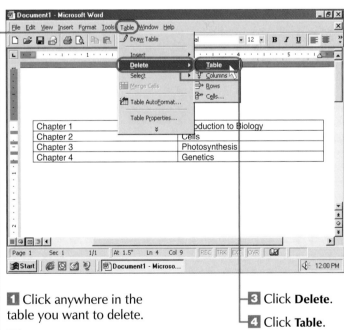

ENTER TEXT IN A TABLE

1 Click the cell where you want to enter text. Then type the text.

2 Repeat step 1 until you finish entering all the text.

■ You can format text in a table as you would format any text in a document. To format text, see pages 74 to 83.

1 Click anywhere in the table you want to delete.

2 Click **Table**.

3 Click **Delete**.

4 Click **Table**.

ADD A ROW OR COLUMN

You can add a row or column to your table when you want to insert additional information.

ADD A ROW

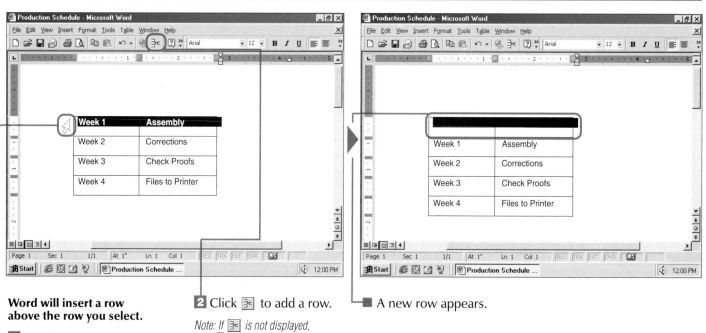

Word will insert a row above the row you select.

1 To select a row, position the mouse I to the left of the row (I changes to ⇗). Then click to select the row.

2 Click ⌹ to add a row.

Note: If ⌹ is not displayed, click ⌹ on the Standard toolbar to display all the buttons.

■ A new row appears.

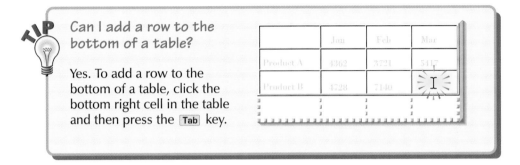

Can I add a row to the bottom of a table?

Yes. To add a row to the bottom of a table, click the bottom right cell in the table and then press the `Tab` key.

ADD A COLUMN

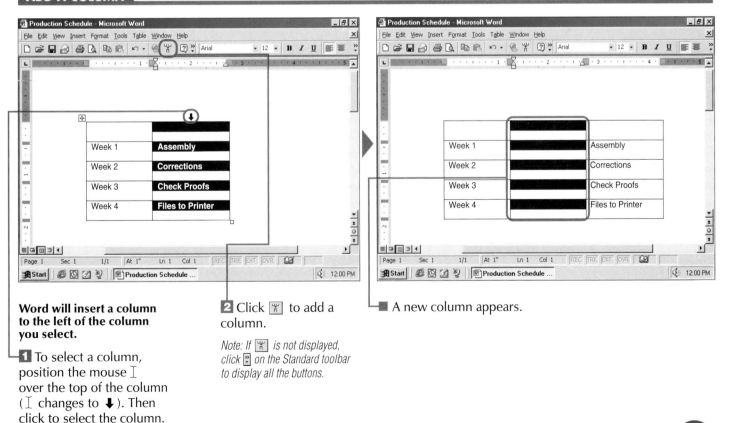

Word will insert a column to the left of the column you select.

1 To select a column, position the mouse I over the top of the column (I changes to ↓). Then click to select the column.

2 Click ⚒ to add a column.

Note: If ⚒ is not displayed, click ⚐ on the Standard toolbar to display all the buttons.

■ A new column appears.

DELETE A ROW OR COLUMN

You can delete a row or column that you no longer need from your table.

When deleting a row or column, the Clipboard toolbar may appear. To hide the Clipboard toolbar, see page 38.

DELETE A ROW

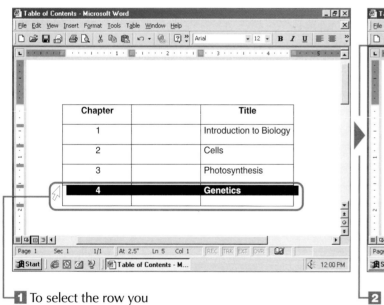

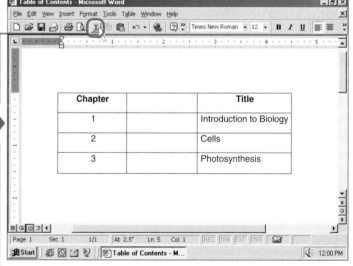

1 To select the row you want to delete, position the mouse I to the left of the row (I changes to ⬦). Then click to select the row.

2 Click ✂ to delete the row.

Note: If ✂ is not displayed, click ░ on the Standard toolbar to display all the buttons.

■ The row disappears.

TIP

Can I delete the information in a row or column without removing the row or column from my table?

Yes. To select the cells displaying the information you want to delete, drag the mouse I over the cells. Then press the Delete key to delete the information.

Movies R Us

Top 8 Movies.

Western	Old Wild West	$13.99
Comedy	Back from Texas	$14.
Comedy	Radio CNTR	$
Drama	Golden Fields	
Horror	Last Night Alive	
Science Fiction	Moon Rock	$18.99
The Classics	Road to Jericho	$14.99
Western	Dusty Roads	$14.99

DELETE A COLUMN

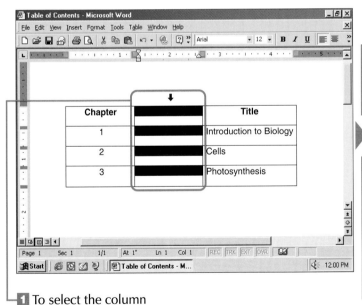

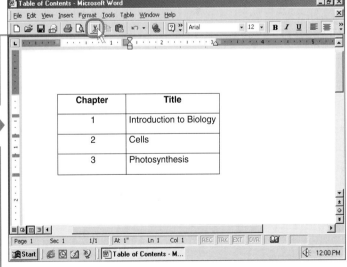

■ 1 To select the column you want to delete, position the mouse I over the top of the column (I changes to ↓). Then click to select the column.

2 Click ✂ to delete the column.

Note: If ✂ is not displayed, click » on the Standard toolbar to display all the buttons.

■ The column disappears.

CHANGE COLUMN WIDTH OR ROW HEIGHT

After you create a table, you can change the width of columns and the height of rows.

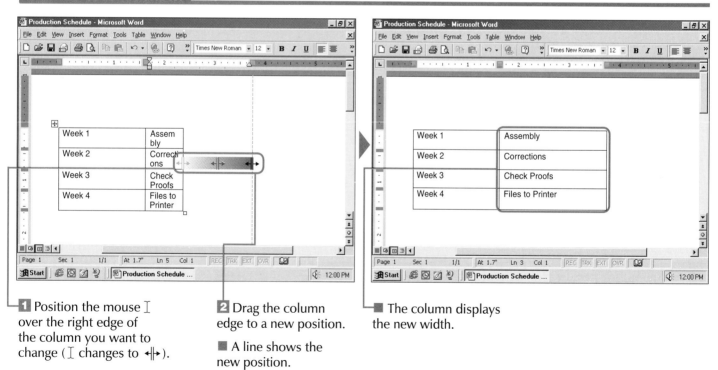

1 Position the mouse I over the right edge of the column you want to change (I changes to ↔).

2 Drag the column edge to a new position.

■ A line shows the new position.

■ The column displays the new width.

TIP

Does Word ever automatically adjust the column width or row height?

When you enter text in a table, Word may automatically increase the width of a column or the height of a row to accommodate the text you type.

CHANGE ROW HEIGHT

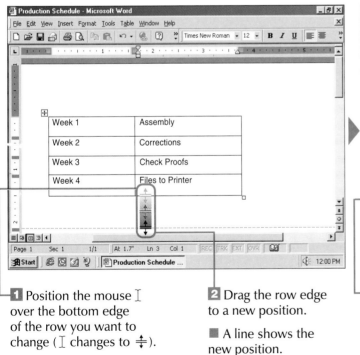

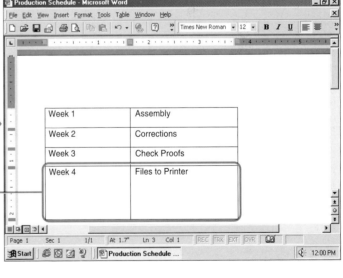

1 Position the mouse I over the bottom edge of the row you want to change (I changes to ↕).

2 Drag the row edge to a new position.

■ A line shows the new position.

■ The row displays the new height.

Note: You cannot change the row height in the Normal or Outline view. For information on the views, see page 34.

MERGE CELLS

You can combine two or more cells in your table to create one large cell. This is useful when you want to display a title in a cell at the top of your table.

MERGE CELLS

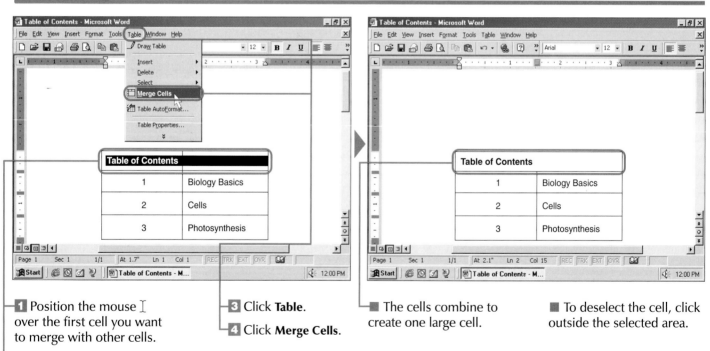

1 Position the mouse I over the first cell you want to merge with other cells.

2 Drag the mouse I until you highlight all the cells you want to merge.

3 Click **Table**.

4 Click **Merge Cells**.

■ The cells combine to create one large cell.

■ To deselect the cell, click outside the selected area.

162

SPLIT CELLS

You can split one cell in your table into several smaller cells.

SPLIT CELLS

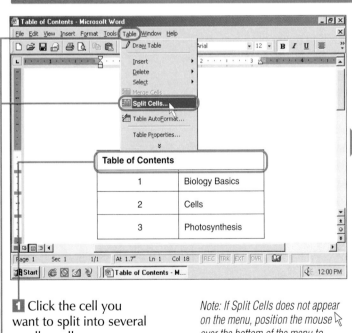

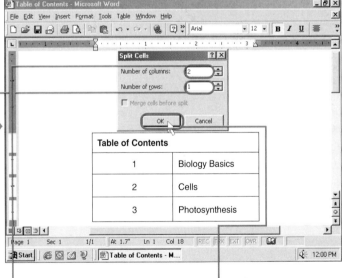

1 Click the cell you want to split into several smaller cells.

2 Click **Table**.

3 Click **Split Cells**.

Note: If Split Cells does not appear on the menu, position the mouse over the bottom of the menu to display all the menu commands.

■ The Split Cells dialog box appears.

4 Double-click this area and then type the number of columns you want to split the cell into.

5 Double-click this area and then type the number of rows you want to split the cell into.

6 Click **OK** to split the cell.

■ The cell splits into the number of columns and rows you specified.

You can enhance the appearance of your table by changing the position of text in cells.

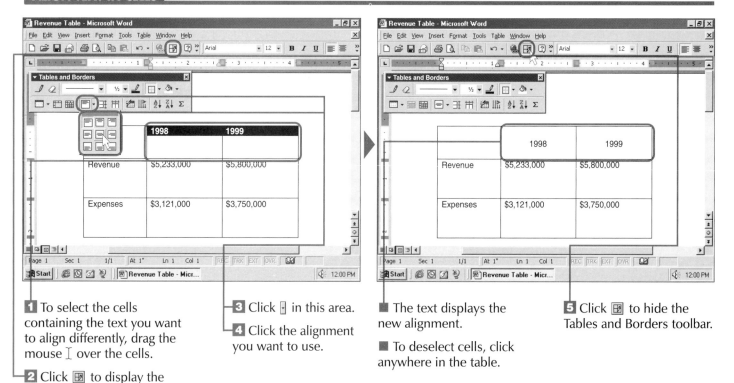

1 To select the cells containing the text you want to align differently, drag the mouse I over the cells.

2 Click to display the Tables and Borders toolbar.

Note: If is not displayed, click on the Standard toolbar to display all the buttons.

3 Click in this area.

4 Click the alignment you want to use.

■ The text displays the new alignment.

■ To deselect cells, click anywhere in the table.

5 Click to hide the Tables and Borders toolbar.

CHANGE TEXT DIRECTION

You can change the direction of text in cells. This can help emphasize row and column headings in your table.

Word can only display the new text direction in the Print Layout and Web Layout views. For more information on the views, see page 34.

CHANGE TEXT DIRECTION

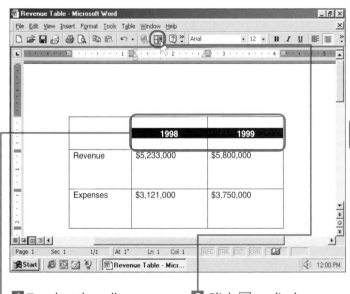

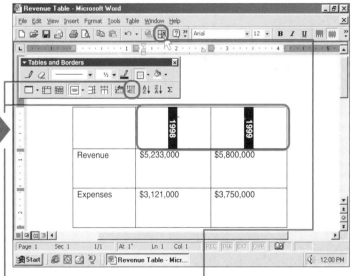

1 To select the cells containing the text you want to change to a new direction, drag the mouse I over the cells.

2 Click to display the Tables and Borders toolbar.

Note: If is not displayed, click on the Standard toolbar to display all the buttons.

3 Click to change the direction of the text. Repeat this step until the text appears the way you want.

■ The text appears in the new direction.

■ To deselect cells, click anywhere in the table.

4 Click to hide the Tables and Borders toolbar.

165

FORMAT A TABLE

Word offers many ready-to-use designs that you can choose from to give your table a new appearance.

FORMAT A TABLE

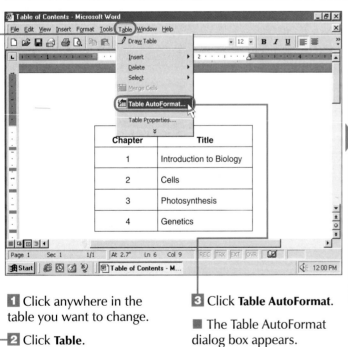

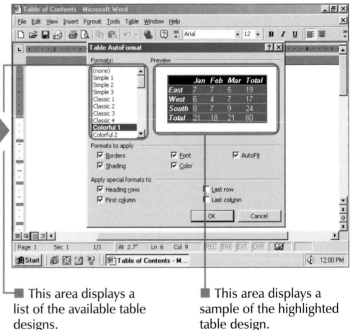

1 Click anywhere in the table you want to change.

2 Click **Table**.

3 Click **Table AutoFormat**.

■ The Table AutoFormat dialog box appears.

■ This area displays a list of the available table designs.

■ This area displays a sample of the highlighted table design.

4 Press the ↓ or ↑ key until the table design you want to use appears.

166

What is the AutoFit option used for?

The AutoFit option changes the size of your table based on the amount of text in the table. If you do not want Word to change the size of your table, you can turn off the AutoFit option in step **5** below (☑ changes to ☐).

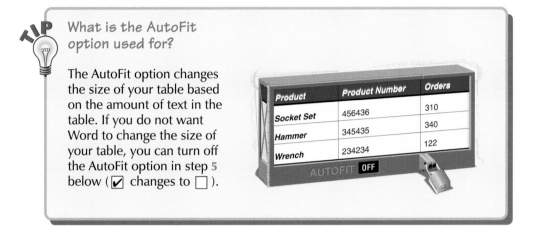

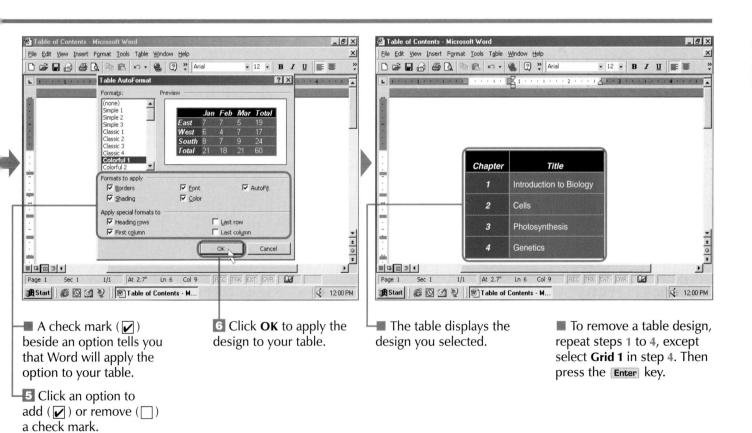

■ A check mark (☑) beside an option tells you that Word will apply the option to your table.

5 Click an option to add (☑) or remove (☐) a check mark.

6 Click **OK** to apply the design to your table.

■ The table displays the design you selected.

■ To remove a table design, repeat steps **1** to **4**, except select **Grid 1** in step **4**. Then press the ⌗Enter⌗ key.

MOVE A TABLE

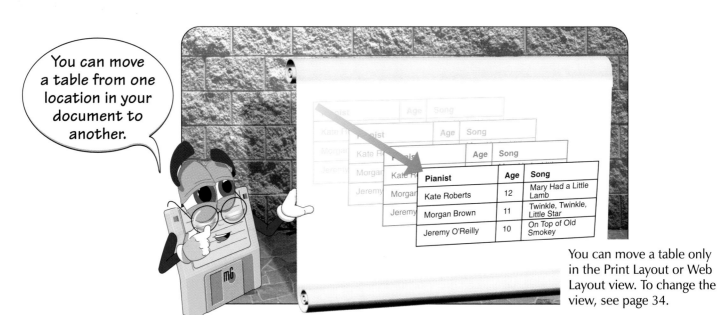

You can move a table from one location in your document to another.

You can move a table only in the Print Layout or Web Layout view. To change the view, see page 34.

MOVE A TABLE

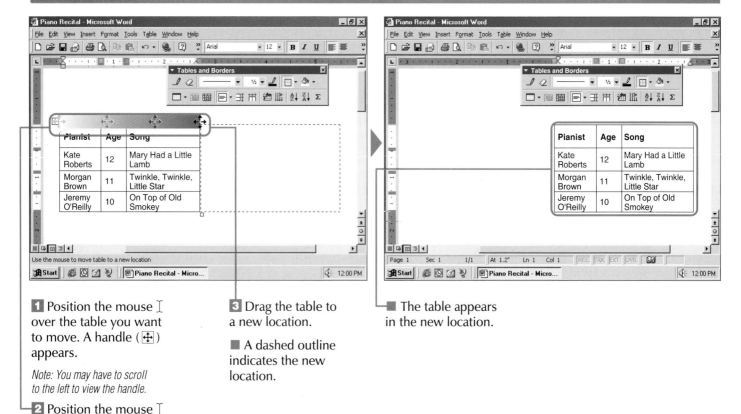

1 Position the mouse I over the table you want to move. A handle (⊞) appears.

Note: You may have to scroll to the left to view the handle.

2 Position the mouse I over the handle (I changes to ✛).

3 Drag the table to a new location.

■ A dashed outline indicates the new location.

■ The table appears in the new location.

SIZE A TABLE

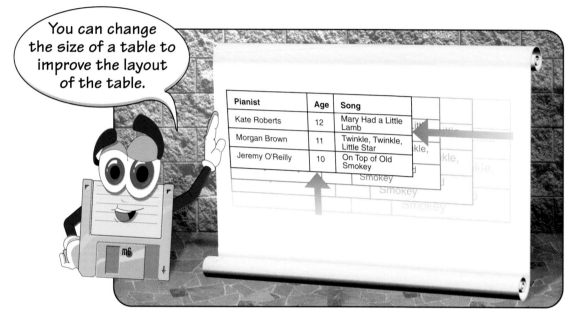

You can change the size of a table to improve the layout of the table.

You can size a table only in the Print Layout or Web Layout view. To change the view, see page 34.

SIZE A TABLE

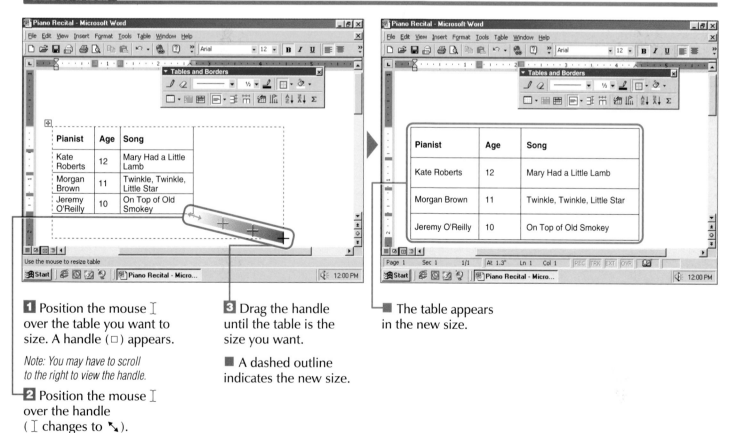

1 Position the mouse I over the table you want to size. A handle (□) appears.

Note: You may have to scroll to the right to view the handle.

2 Position the mouse I over the handle (I changes to ↖).

3 Drag the handle until the table is the size you want.

■ A dashed outline indicates the new size.

■ The table appears in the new size.

CHAPTER 10

WORK WITH GRAPHICS

Are you interested in using graphics to enhance the appearance of your document? This chapter shows you how.

TEXT EFFECTS

Word provides many ready-made shapes, called AutoShapes, that you can add to your document.

Word can only display AutoShapes in the Print Layout and Web Layout views. For more information on the views, see page 34.

ADD AN AUTOSHAPE

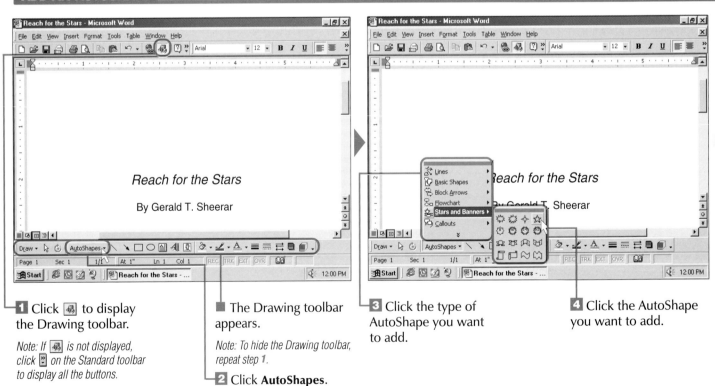

1 Click ![icon] to display the Drawing toolbar.

Note: If ![icon] is not displayed, click ![icon] on the Standard toolbar to display all the buttons.

■ The Drawing toolbar appears.

Note: To hide the Drawing toolbar, repeat step 1.

2 Click **AutoShapes**.

3 Click the type of AutoShape you want to add.

4 Click the AutoShape you want to add.

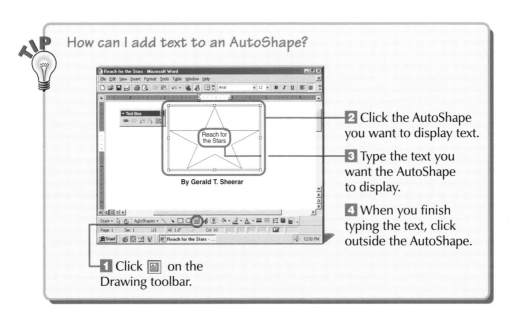

How can I add text to an AutoShape?

2 Click the AutoShape you want to display text.

3 Type the text you want the AutoShape to display.

4 When you finish typing the text, click outside the AutoShape.

1 Click 🔲 on the Drawing toolbar.

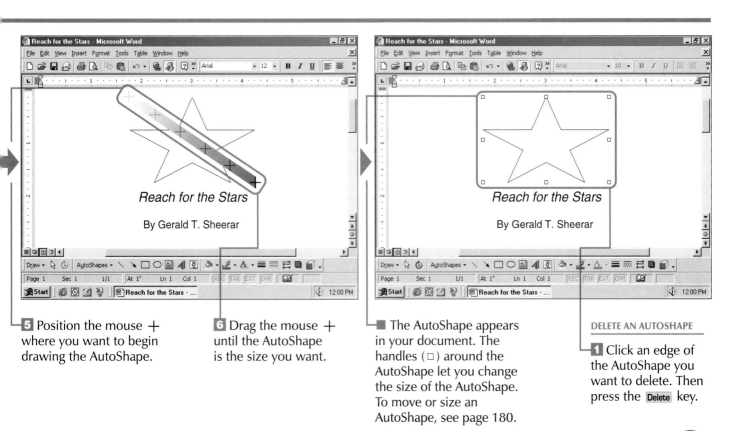

5 Position the mouse ✛ where you want to begin drawing the AutoShape.

6 Drag the mouse ✛ until the AutoShape is the size you want.

■ The AutoShape appears in your document. The handles (□) around the AutoShape let you change the size of the AutoShape. To move or size an AutoShape, see page 180.

7 To hide the handles, click outside the AutoShape.

DELETE AN AUTOSHAPE

1 Click an edge of the AutoShape you want to delete. Then press the `Delete` key.

173

You can use the WordArt feature to add a text effect to your document. Text effects can enhance the appearance of a title or draw attention to important information.

Word can only display text effects in the Print Layout and Web Layout views. For more information on the views, see page 34.

ADD A TEXT EFFECT

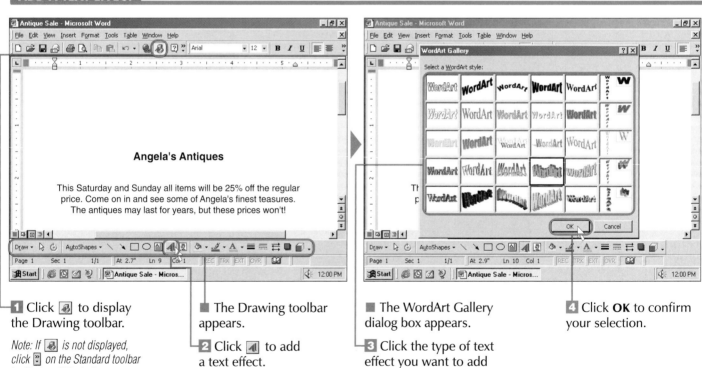

1 Click to display the Drawing toolbar.

Note: If is not displayed, click on the Standard toolbar to display all the buttons.

■ The Drawing toolbar appears.

2 Click to add a text effect.

■ The WordArt Gallery dialog box appears.

3 Click the type of text effect you want to add to your document.

4 Click **OK** to confirm your selection.

How do I edit a text effect?

Double-click the text effect to display the Edit WordArt Text dialog box. Then edit the text in the dialog box. When you finish editing the text effect, click **OK** to display the changes in your document.

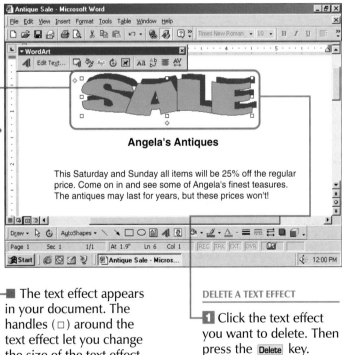

■ The Edit WordArt Text dialog box appears.

5 Type the text you want the text effect to display.

6 Click **OK** to add the text effect to your document.

■ The text effect appears in your document. The handles (□) around the text effect let you change the size of the text effect. To move or size a text effect, see page 180.

7 To hide the handles, click outside the text effect.

Note: To hide the Drawing toolbar, repeat step 1.

DELETE A TEXT EFFECT

1 Click the text effect you want to delete. Then press the Delete key.

Word includes professionally designed clip art images that you can add to your document. Clip art images can help illustrate concepts and make your document more interesting.

Word provides thousands of clip art images that you can choose from.

ADD CLIP ART

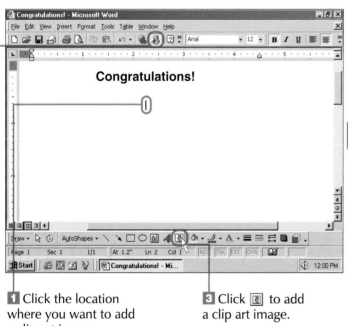

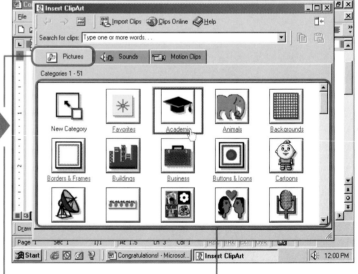

1 Click the location where you want to add a clip art image.

2 Click 🖳 to display the Drawing toolbar.

Note: If 🖳 is not displayed, click ➤ on the Standard toolbar to display all the buttons.

3 Click 🖳 to add a clip art image.

■ The Insert ClipArt window appears.

4 Click the **Pictures** tab.

5 Click the category of clip art images you want to display.

■ The clip art images in the category you selected appear.

Where can I find more clip art images?

If you are connected to the Internet, you can visit Microsoft's Clip Gallery Live Web site to find additional clip art images. In the Insert ClipArt window, click **Clips Online**. In the dialog box that appears, click **OK** to connect to the Web site.

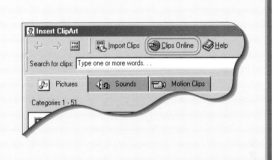

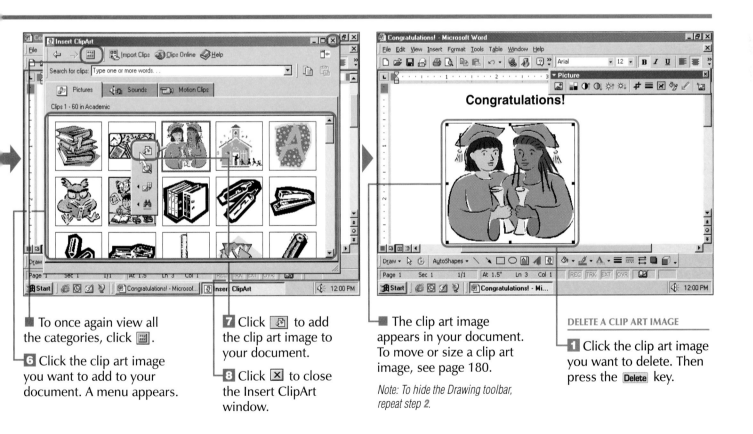

■ To once again view all the categories, click 🔲.

6 Click the clip art image you want to add to your document. A menu appears.

7 Click 🔲 to add the clip art image to your document.

8 Click ☒ to close the Insert ClipArt window.

■ The clip art image appears in your document. To move or size a clip art image, see page 180.

Note: To hide the Drawing toolbar, repeat step 2.

DELETE A CLIP ART IMAGE

1 Click the clip art image you want to delete. Then press the Delete key.

You can add a picture stored on your computer to your document.

Adding a picture is useful if you want to display your company logo or a picture of your family in your document.

ADD A PICTURE

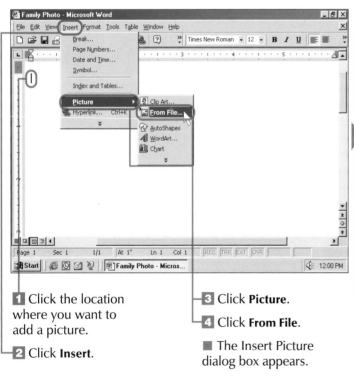

1 Click the location where you want to add a picture.

2 Click **Insert**.

3 Click **Picture**.

4 Click **From File**.

■ The Insert Picture dialog box appears.

■ This area shows the location of the displayed files. You can click this area to change the location.

■ This area allows you to access commonly used folders. To display the contents of a folder, click the folder.

Note: For information on the commonly used folders, see the top of page 23.

178

TIP

Where can I get pictures that I can use in my documents?

You can use a drawing program to create your own pictures or use a scanner to scan pictures into your computer. You can also find collections of pictures at most computer stores and on the Internet.

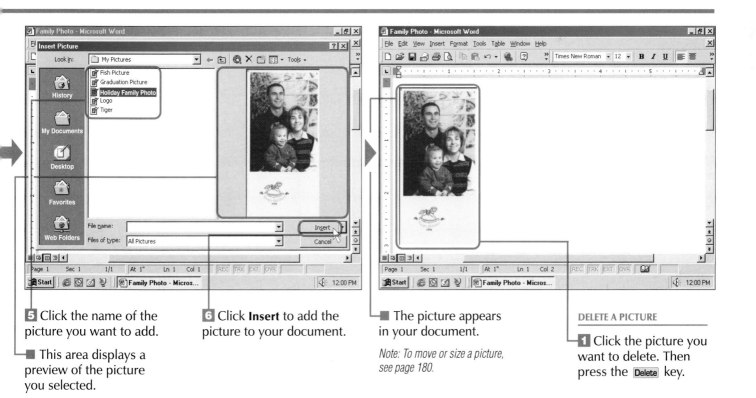

5 Click the name of the picture you want to add.

■ This area displays a preview of the picture you selected.

6 Click **Insert** to add the picture to your document.

■ The picture appears in your document.

Note: To move or size a picture, see page 180.

DELETE A PICTURE

1 Click the picture you want to delete. Then press the Delete key.

You can change the location or size of a graphic in your document.

- MOVE -

- SIZE -

Word can display graphics in the Print Layout and Web Layout views. For more information on the views, see page 34.

MOVE A GRAPHIC

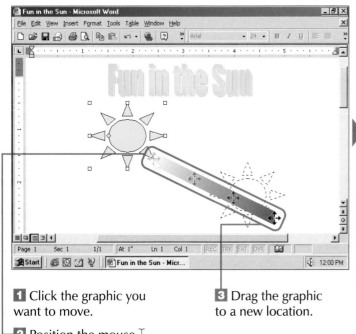

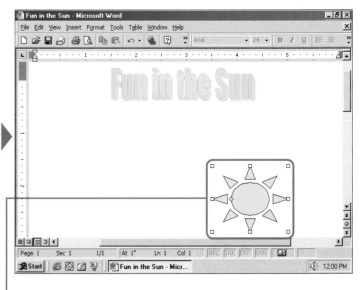

1 Click the graphic you want to move.

2 Position the mouse I over the graphic (I changes to ✛ or ↖).

3 Drag the graphic to a new location.

■ The graphic appears in the new location.

Note: If you have problems moving a graphic, see page 182 to change the way text wraps around the graphic. This will give you more control over the placement of the graphic.

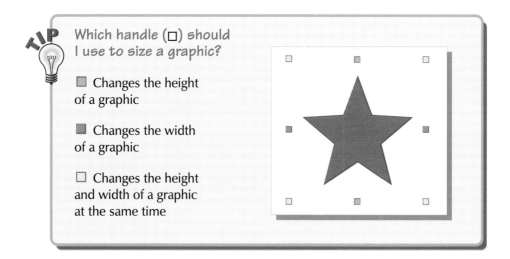

Which handle (□) should
I use to size a graphic?

■ Changes the height
of a graphic

■ Changes the width
of a graphic

□ Changes the height
and width of a graphic
at the same time

SIZE A GRAPHIC

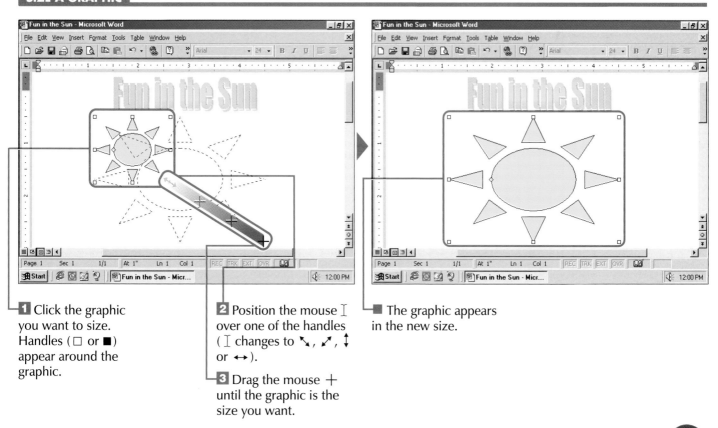

1 Click the graphic
you want to size.
Handles (□ or ■)
appear around the
graphic.

2 Position the mouse I
over one of the handles
(I changes to ↘ , ↗ , ↕
or ↔).

3 Drag the mouse +
until the graphic is the
size you want.

■ The graphic appears
in the new size.

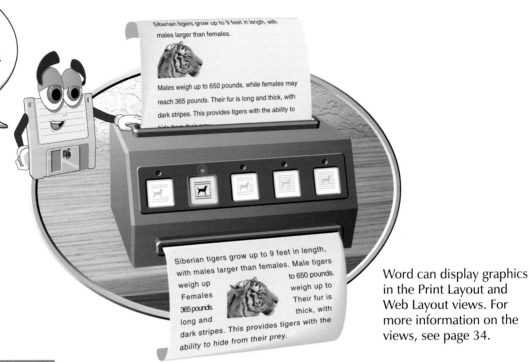

After you add a graphic to your document, you can choose how you want to wrap text around the graphic.

Word can display graphics in the Print Layout and Web Layout views. For more information on the views, see page 34.

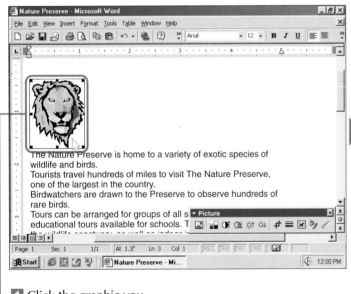

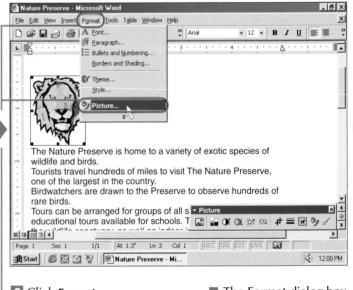

1 Click the graphic you want to wrap text around.

2 Click **Format**.

3 Click the command for the type of graphic you selected, such as **AutoShape**, **Picture** or **WordArt**.

■ The Format dialog box appears.

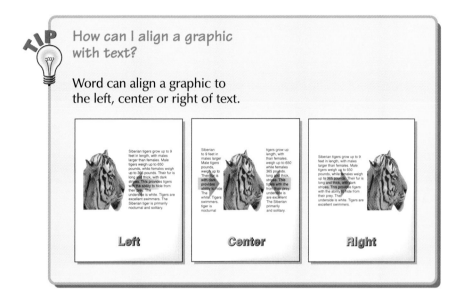

How can I align a graphic with text?

Word can align a graphic to the left, center or right of text.

Left

Center

Right

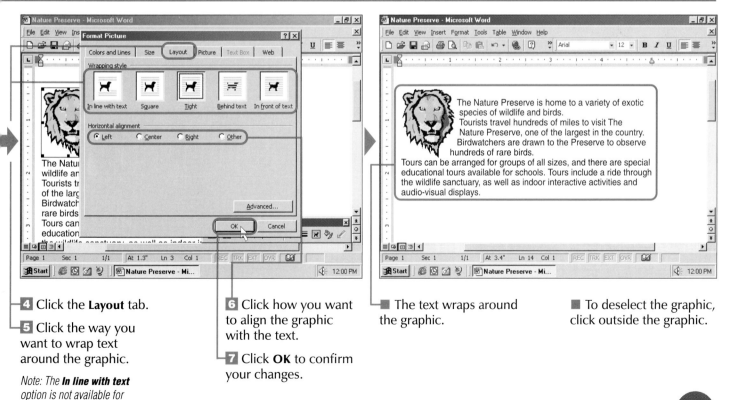

■4 Click the **Layout** tab.

■5 Click the way you want to wrap text around the graphic.

*Note: The **In line with text** option is not available for some types of graphics.*

■6 Click how you want to align the graphic with the text.

■7 Click **OK** to confirm your changes.

■ The text wraps around the graphic.

■ To deselect the graphic, click outside the graphic.

CHAPTER 11

MAIL MERGE

Would you like to quickly produce a personalized letter for each person on a mailing list? This chapter teaches you how.

Performing a mail merge is useful if you often send the same document, such as an announcement or advertisement, to many people.

Create a Main Document

A main document is a letter you want to send to each person on your mailing list.

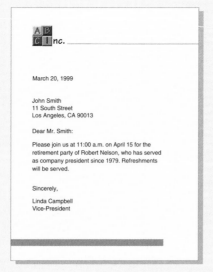

Create a Data Source

A data source contains the information that changes in each letter, such as the name and address of each person on your mailing list. You only need to create a data source once. After you create a data source, you can use the data source in future mailings. A data source consists of fields and records.

FirstName	LastName	Address	City	State	PostalCode
Ted	Duxan	14 Pine Street	Los Angeles	CA	90023
John	Smith	11 South Street	Los Angeles	CA	90013
Heather	Brown	56 Maple Street	San Diego	CA	92128
Jim	Hunter	14 Willow Avenue	Los Angeles	CA	90028
Linda	Wilson	989 Main Street	Burbank	CA	91505
Ted	Green	66 River Road	Burbank	CA	91501

Field

A field is a specific category of information. Each field has a name, such as LastName or City.

Record

A record is all the information for one person on your mailing list.

TIP

What types of documents can I create using the Mail Merge feature?

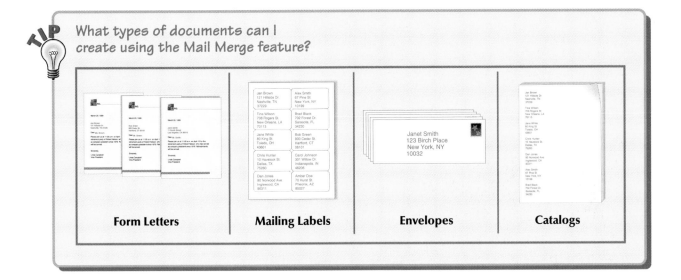

| Form Letters | Mailing Labels | Envelopes | Catalogs |

Complete the Main Document

To complete the main document, you must insert special instructions into the main document. These instructions tell Word where to place the personalized information from the data source.

Merge the Main Document and Data Source

You combine, or merge, the main document and the data source to create a personalized letter for each person on your mailing list. Word replaces the special instructions in the main document with the personalized information from the data source.

The main document contains the text that remains the same in each letter.

March 22, 1999

Dear _____ :

Please join us at 11:00 a.m. on April 15 for the retirement party of Robert Nelson, who has served as company president since 1979. Refreshments will be served.

Sincerely,

Linda Campbell
Vice-President

CREATE A MAIN DOCUMENT

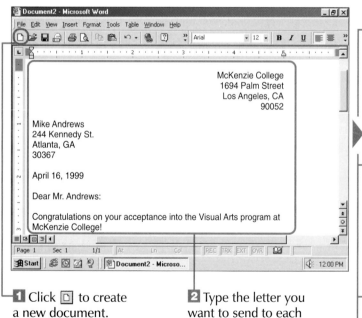

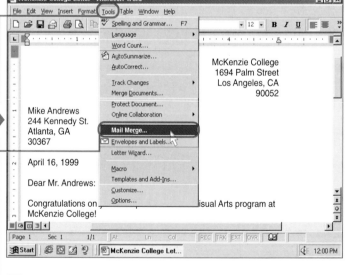

1 Click ▯ to create a new document.

Note: If ▯ is not displayed, click ▯ on the Standard toolbar to display all the buttons.

2 Type the letter you want to send to each person on your mailing list. Include the information for one person.

3 Save the document. To save a document, see page 22.

4 Click **Tools**.

5 Click **Mail Merge**.

Note: If Mail Merge does not appear on the menu, position the mouse ▯ over the bottom of the menu to display all the menu commands.

■ The Mail Merge Helper dialog box appears.

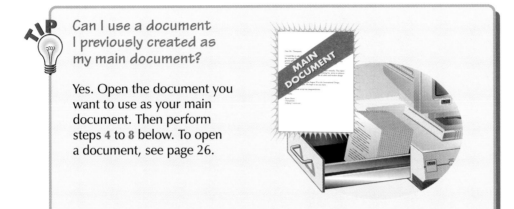

TIP

Can I use a document I previously created as my main document?

Yes. Open the document you want to use as your main document. Then perform steps 4 to 8 below. To open a document, see page 26.

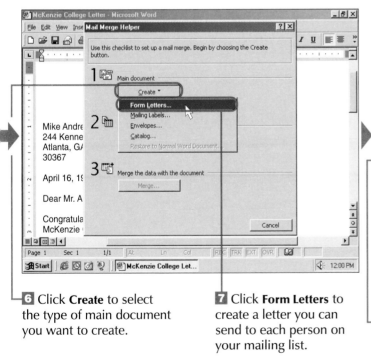

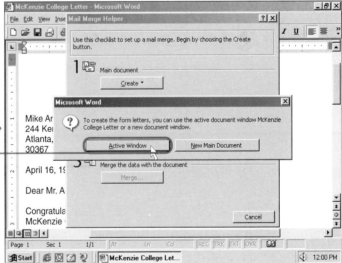

6 Click **Create** to select the type of main document you want to create.

7 Click **Form Letters** to create a letter you can send to each person on your mailing list.

■ A dialog box appears.

8 Click **Active Window** to make the document displayed on your screen the main document.

■ To continue, you must create a data source or open an existing data source. To create a data source, see page 190. To open an existing data source, see page 196.

The data source contains the personalized information that changes in each letter, such as the name and address of each person on your mailing list.

You only need to create a data source once. To open an existing data source, see page 196.

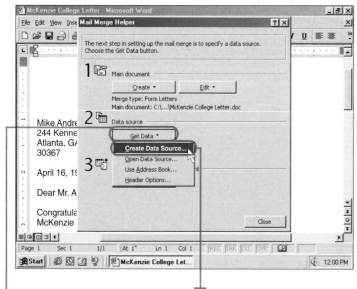

■ Before creating a data source, you must create a main document. To create a main document, see page 188.

1 Click **Get Data**.

2 Click **Create Data Source**.

■ The Create Data Source dialog box appears.

■ Word provides a list of commonly used field names.

3 To remove a field name you do not need, click the field name.

4 Click **Remove Field Name**.

■ The field name disappears from the list.

What is a field name?

A field name is a name given to a category of information, such as LastName or City. When you create a data source, Word provides a list of field names you can choose from. You can remove and add field names until you have all the field names you need.

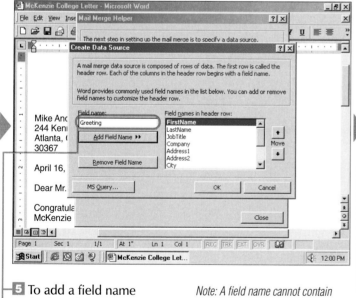

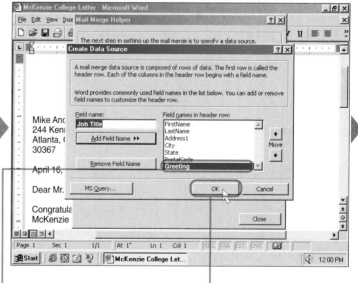

5 To add a field name to the list, double-click this area.

6 Type the field name and then press the Enter key.

Note: A field name cannot contain spaces and must begin with a letter.

■ The field name appears in the list.

7 Remove and add field names until the list displays the field names you want to use.

8 Click **OK** to continue.

CONTINUED

After you save the data source, you can enter the information for each person on your mailing list.

CREATE A DATA SOURCE (CONTINUED)

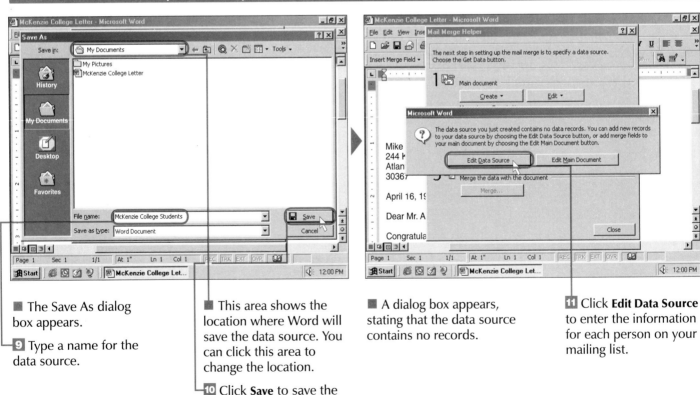

■ The Save As dialog box appears.

9 Type a name for the data source.

■ This area shows the location where Word will save the data source. You can click this area to change the location.

10 Click **Save** to save the data source.

■ A dialog box appears, stating that the data source contains no records.

11 Click **Edit Data Source** to enter the information for each person on your mailing list.

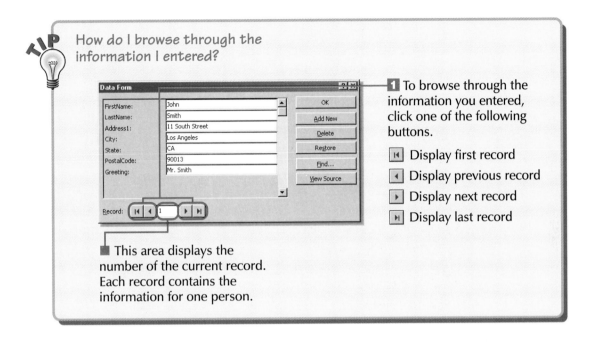

How do I browse through the information I entered?

1 To browse through the information you entered, click one of the following buttons.

|◄ Display first record

◄ Display previous record

► Display next record

►| Display last record

■ This area displays the number of the current record. Each record contains the information for one person.

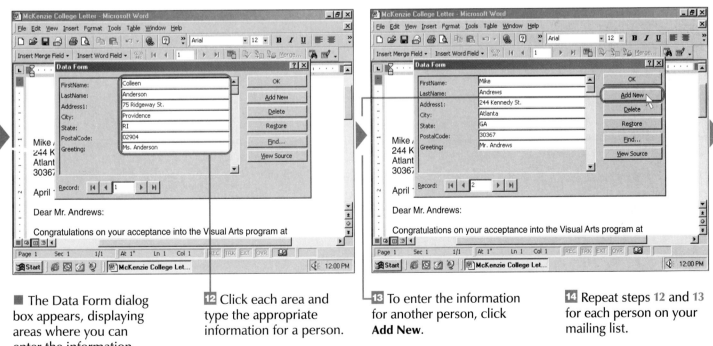

■ The Data Form dialog box appears, displaying areas where you can enter the information for a person on your mailing list.

12 Click each area and type the appropriate information for a person.

13 To enter the information for another person, click **Add New**.

14 Repeat steps 12 and 13 for each person on your mailing list.

CONTINUED

When you finish entering information in the data source, you can display a table showing all the information you entered.

FirstName	LastName	Address1	City	State	PostalCode
John	Smith	11 South Street	Los Angeles	CA	90013
Heather	Brown	56 Maple Street	San Diego	CA	92128
Jim	Hunter	14 Willow Avenue	Los Angeles	CA	90028
	Wilson	989 Main Street	Burbank	CA	91505
Green	...ver Road		Burbank	CA	91501

CREATE A DATA SOURCE (CONTINUED)

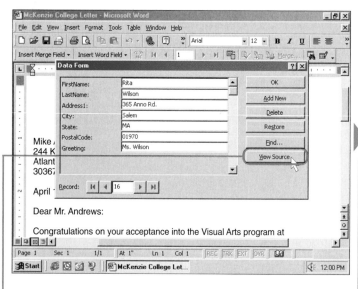

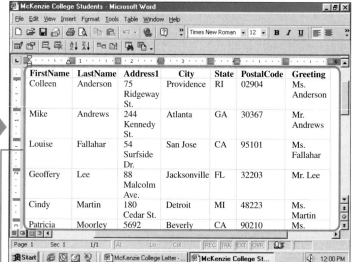

15 When you finish entering the information for all the people on your mailing list, click **View Source**.

■ The information you entered appears in a table.

■ The first row in the table displays the field names you specified. Each of the following rows displays the information for one person.

Note: Text that does not fit on one line in the table will appear on one line when you print the letters.

194

How do I change information in my data source?

When viewing the data source, you can click  to redisplay the Data Form dialog box. You can then add or change information for people on your mailing list. You can also edit the text directly in the table as you would edit any text in a document.

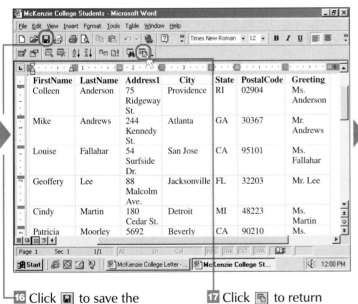

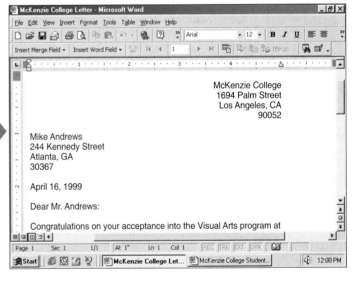

16 Click 🖫 to save the information you entered.

Note: If 🖫 is not displayed, click ▾ on the Standard toolbar to display all the buttons.

17 Click 🖹 to return to the main document.

■ The main document appears on your screen.

■ To continue, you must complete the main document. To complete the main document, see page 198.

You can use a data source you previously created to perform a mail merge.

A data source contains the information that changes in each letter, such as the name and address of each person on your mailing list.

OPEN AN EXISTING DATA SOURCE

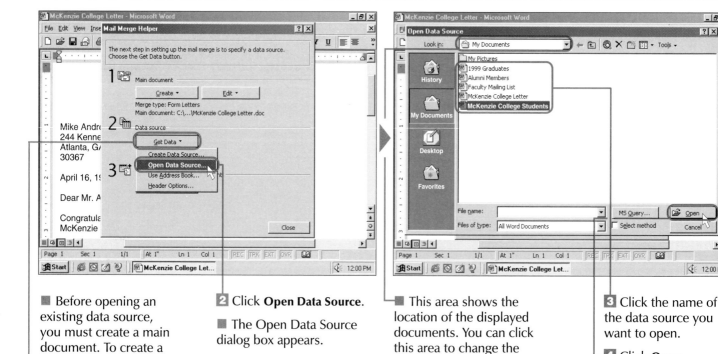

■ Before opening an existing data source, you must create a main document. To create a main document, see page 188.

1 Click **Get Data**.

2 Click **Open Data Source**.

■ The Open Data Source dialog box appears.

■ This area shows the location of the displayed documents. You can click this area to change the location.

3 Click the name of the data source you want to open.

4 Click **Open**.

196

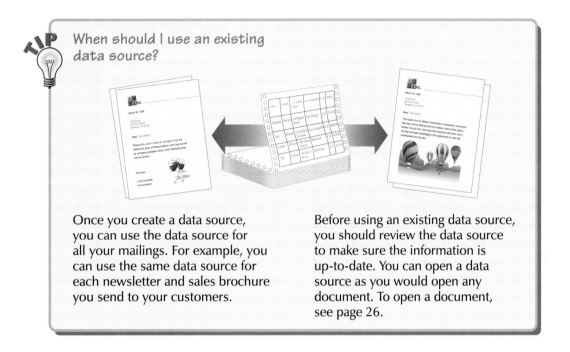

TIP

When should I use an existing data source?

Once you create a data source, you can use the data source for all your mailings. For example, you can use the same data source for each newsletter and sales brochure you send to your customers.

Before using an existing data source, you should review the data source to make sure the information is up-to-date. You can open a data source as you would open any document. To open a document, see page 26.

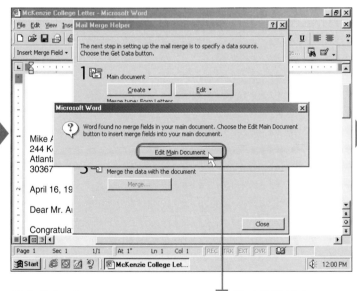

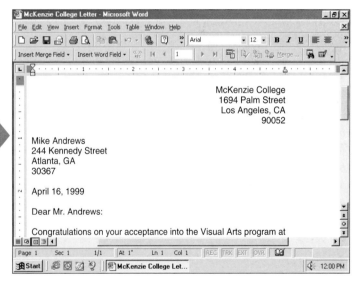

■ A dialog box appears.

5 Click **Edit Main Document** to return to the main document.

■ The main document appears on your screen.

■ To continue, you must complete the main document. To complete the main document, see page 198.

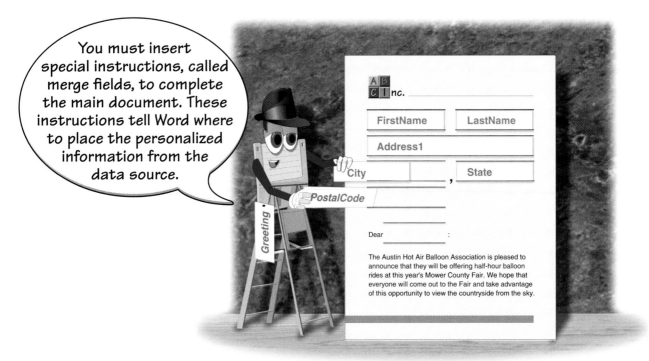

You must insert special instructions, called merge fields, to complete the main document. These instructions tell Word where to place the personalized information from the data source.

COMPLETE THE MAIN DOCUMENT

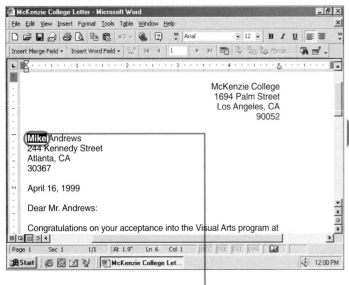

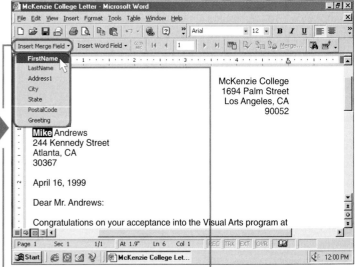

■ Before completing the main document, you must create a main document. To create a main document, see page 188.

1 Select an area of text that you want to change in each letter. Do not select any spaces before or after the text. To select text, see page 14.

2 Click **Insert Merge Field** to display a list of merge fields.

Note: The merge fields that appear depend on the field names you specified when you created the data source.

3 Click the merge field that corresponds to the text you selected in step 1.

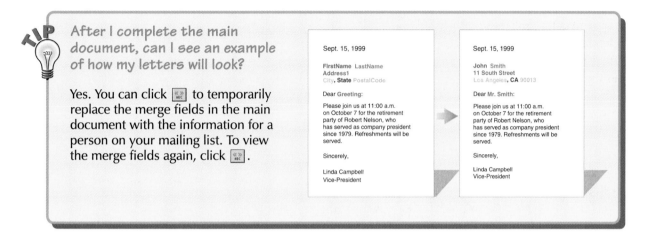

TIP

After I complete the main document, can I see an example of how my letters will look?

Yes. You can click [icon] to temporarily replace the merge fields in the main document with the information for a person on your mailing list. To view the merge fields again, click [icon].

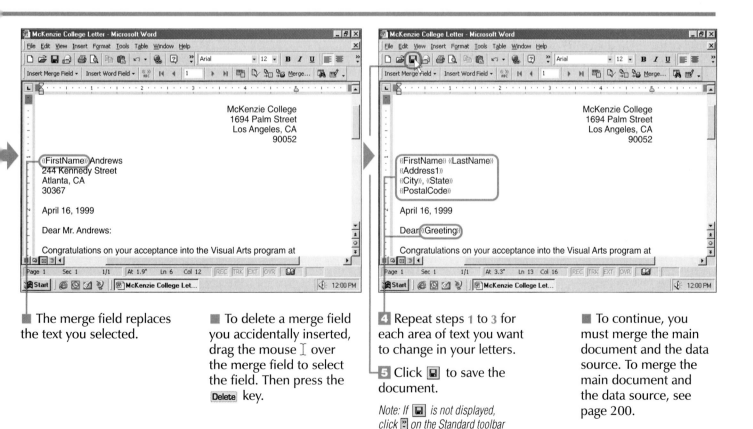

■ The merge field replaces the text you selected.

■ To delete a merge field you accidentally inserted, drag the mouse I over the merge field to select the field. Then press the **Delete** key.

4 Repeat steps **1** to **3** for each area of text you want to change in your letters.

5 Click [icon] to save the document.

Note: If [icon] is not displayed, click [icon] on the Standard toolbar to display all the buttons.

■ To continue, you must merge the main document and the data source. To merge the main document and the data source, see page 200.

You can combine the main document and the data source to create a personalized letter for each person on your mailing list.

MERGE THE MAIN DOCUMENT AND DATA SOURCE

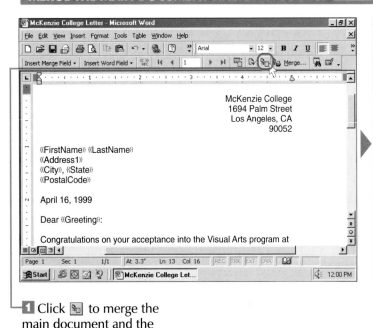

1 Click to merge the main document and the data source.

■ A new document appears, displaying a personalized letter for each person on your mailing list.

■ Word replaced the merge fields in the main document with the corresponding information from the data source.

Should I save the merged document?

To conserve hard disk space, do not save the merged document. You can easily recreate the merged document at any time by opening the main document and then performing step 1 on page 200. To open a document, see page 26.

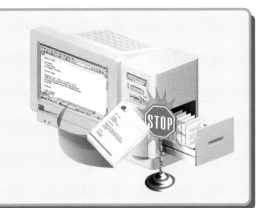

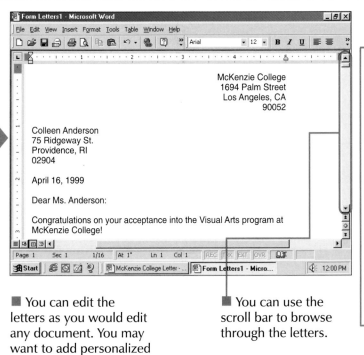

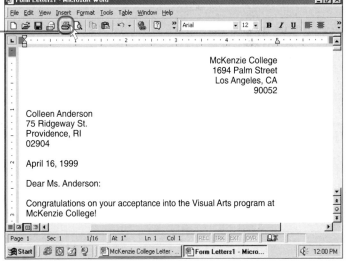

■ You can edit the letters as you would edit any document. You may want to add personalized comments to some letters.

■ You can use the scroll bar to browse through the letters.

PRINT MERGED DOCUMENT

1 When you finish reviewing the letters, click 🖨 to print the letters. To print only some of the letters, see page 136 for more information on printing.

Note: If 🖨 is not displayed, click » on the Standard toolbar to display all the buttons.

You can use the Mail Merge feature to print a personalized label for each person on your mailing list. This saves you from typing each label individually.

You can use labels for addressing envelopes and packages and creating name tags.

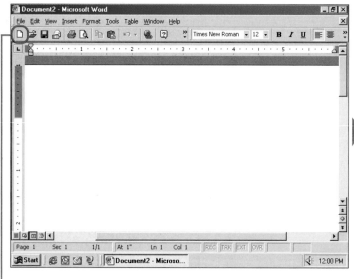

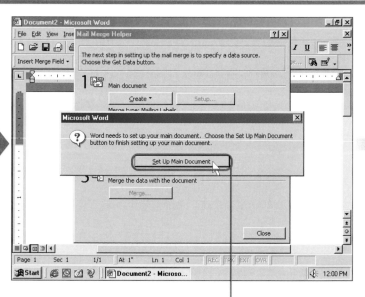

1 Click ☐ to create a new document.

Note: If ☐ is not displayed, click ⏵ on the Standard toolbar to display all the buttons.

2 To tell Word that you want to create labels, perform steps **4** to **8** starting on page 188, except select **Mailing Labels** in step **7**.

3 To open an existing data source, perform steps **1** to **4** on page 196.

4 Click **Set Up Main Document** to set up the labels.

■ The Label Options dialog box appears.

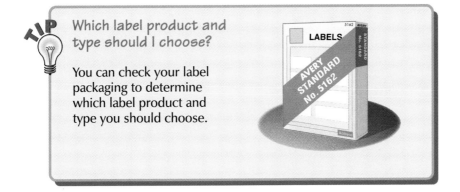

Which label product and type should I choose?

You can check your label packaging to determine which label product and type you should choose.

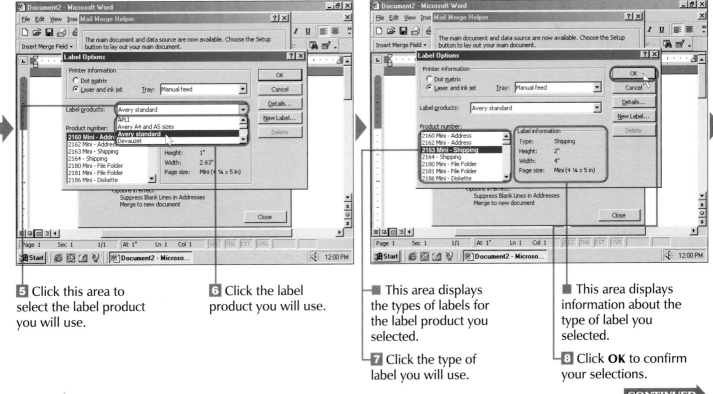

5 Click this area to select the label product you will use.

6 Click the label product you will use.

■ This area displays the types of labels for the label product you selected.

7 Click the type of label you will use.

■ This area displays information about the type of label you selected.

8 Click **OK** to confirm your selections.

CONTINUED

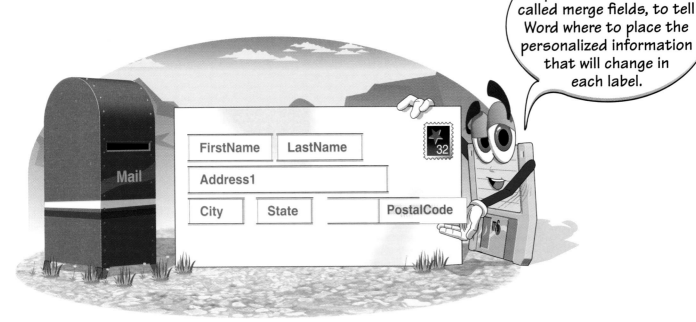

You must insert special instructions, called merge fields, to tell Word where to place the personalized information that will change in each label.

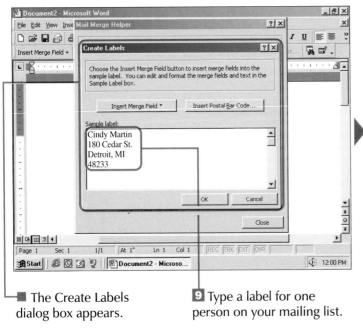

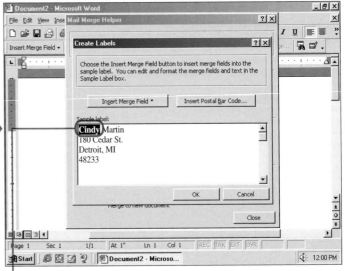

■ The Create Labels dialog box appears.

9 Type a label for one person on your mailing list.

10 Select an area of text that you want to change in each label. Do not select any spaces before or after the text. To select text, see page 14.

TIP

Can I create labels without using the Mail Merge feature?

Yes. You can type the text you want to appear on each label yourself. For information on printing labels without using the Mail Merge feature, see page 140.

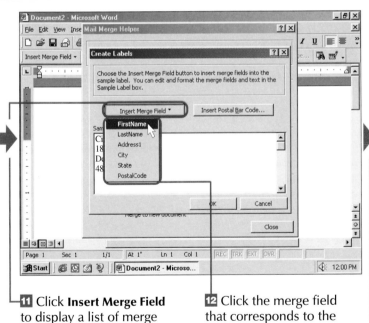

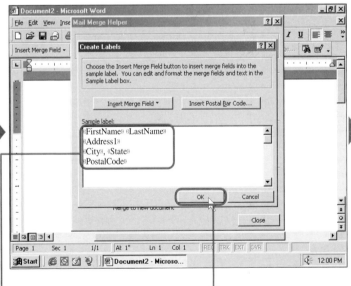

11 Click **Insert Merge Field** to display a list of merge fields.

Note: The merge fields that appear depend on the field names you specified when you created the data source.

12 Click the merge field that corresponds to the text you selected in step **10**.

■ The merge field replaces the text you selected.

13 Repeat steps **10** to **12** for each area of text you want to change in your labels.

14 Click **OK** to continue.

CONTINUED

After you merge the labels and the data source, you can print the personalized labels Word created for each person on your mailing list.

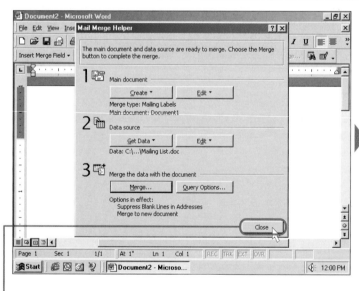

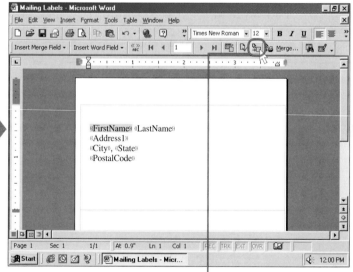

15 Click **Close** to close the Mail Merge Helper dialog box.

■ The labels appear, displaying the merge fields you selected.

16 Save the document. To save a document, see page 22.

17 Click 🔲 to merge the labels and the data source.

Should I save the merged labels?

To conserve hard disk space, do not save the merged labels. You can easily recreate the merged labels at any time by opening the label document you saved in step **16** below and then performing step **17** below. To open a document, see page 26.

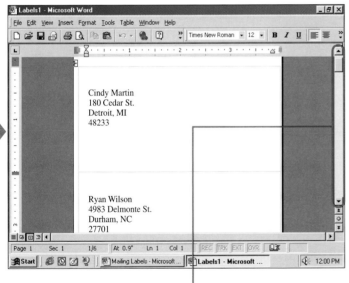

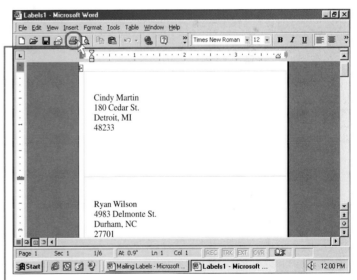

■ A new document appears, displaying a personalized label for each person on your mailing list.

■ You can edit the labels as you would edit any document.

■ You can use the scroll bar to browse through the labels.

PRINT MERGED LABELS

1 When you finish reviewing the labels, click 🖨 to print the labels. To print only some of the labels, see page 136 for more information on printing.

Note: If 🖨 is not displayed, click 🔽 on the Standard toolbar to display all the buttons.

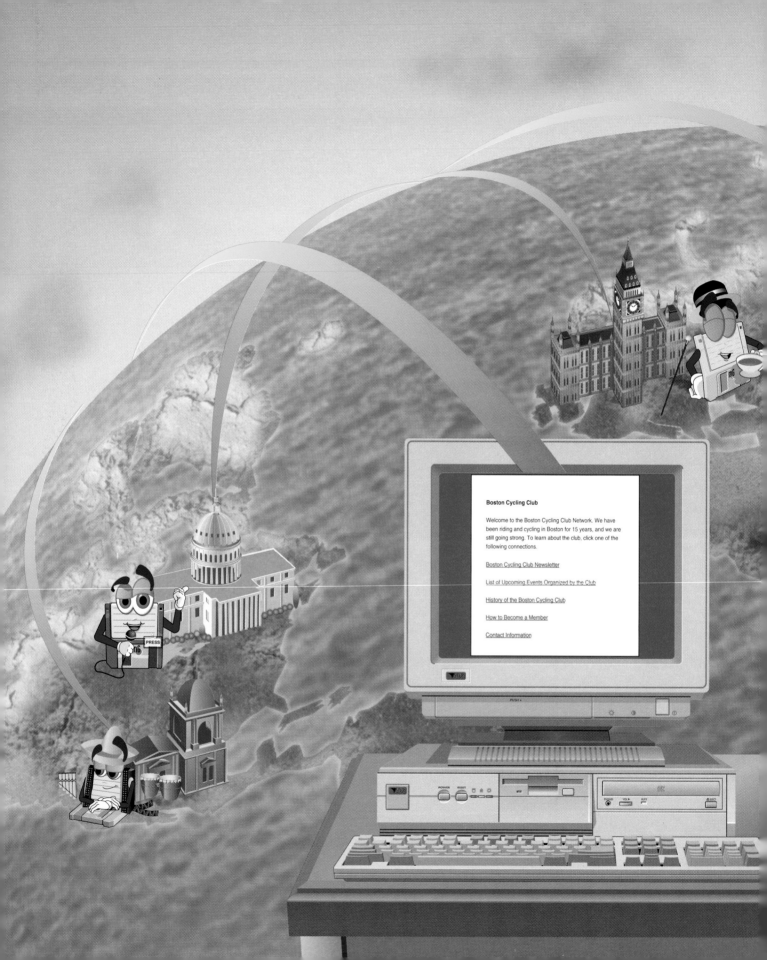

Boston Cycling Club

Welcome to the Boston Cycling Club Network. We have been riding and cycling in Boston for 15 years, and we are still going strong. To learn about the club, click one of the following connections.

Boston Cycling Club Newsletter

List of Upcoming Events Organized by the Club

History of the Boston Cycling Club

How to Become a Member

Contact Information

CHAPTER 12

WORD AND THE INTERNET

Are you wondering how you can use Word to share information with other people on the Internet? In this chapter you will learn how to e-mail a document, save a document as a Web page and more.

You can e-mail the document displayed on your screen to a friend, family member or colleague.

Before you can e-mail a document, Microsoft Outlook must be set up on your computer. Microsoft Outlook is a program that allows you to send and receive e-mail messages.

E-MAIL A DOCUMENT

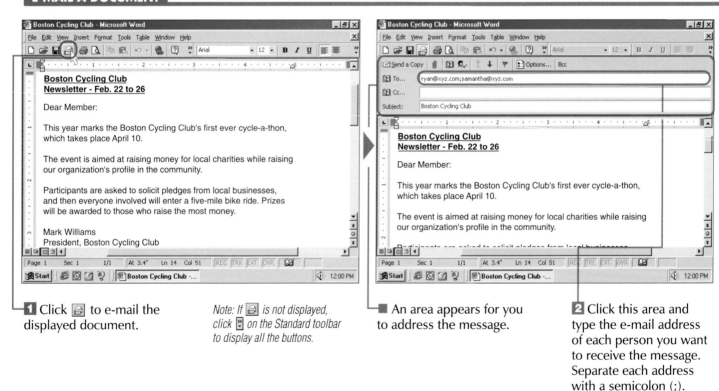

1 Click 📧 to e-mail the displayed document.

Note: If 📧 is not displayed, click ❯❯ on the Standard toolbar to display all the buttons.

■ An area appears for you to address the message.

2 Click this area and type the e-mail address of each person you want to receive the message. Separate each address with a semicolon (;).

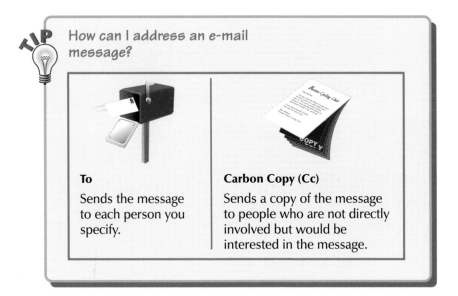

TIP

How can I address an e-mail message?

To

Sends the message to each person you specify.

Carbon Copy (Cc)

Sends a copy of the message to people who are not directly involved but would be interested in the message.

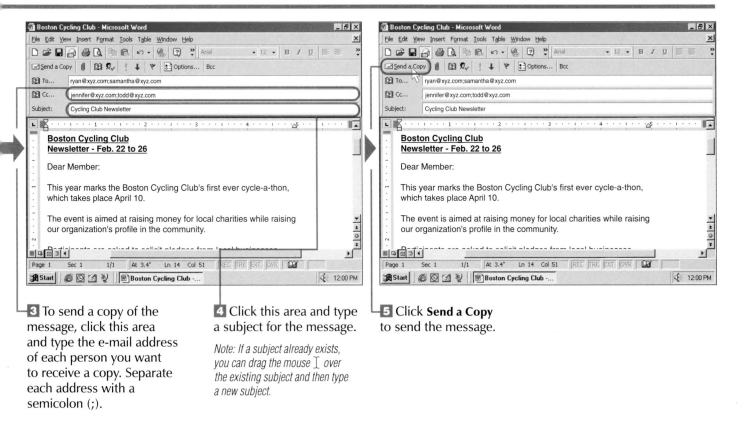

3 To send a copy of the message, click this area and type the e-mail address of each person you want to receive a copy. Separate each address with a semicolon (;).

4 Click this area and type a subject for the message.

Note: If a subject already exists, you can drag the mouse I over the existing subject and then type a new subject.

5 Click **Send a Copy** to send the message.

CREATE A HYPERLINK

> You can create a hyperlink to connect a word or phrase in your document to another document on your computer, network, corporate intranet or the Internet.

An intranet is a small version of the Internet within a company or organization.

CREATE A HYPERLINK

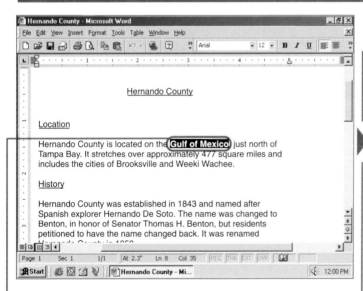

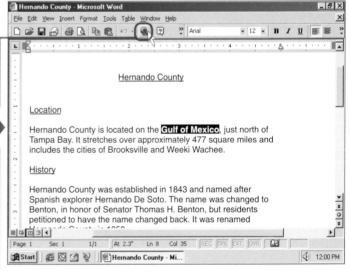

1 Select the text you want to make a hyperlink. To select text, see page 14.

2 Click 🔗 to create a hyperlink.

Note: If 🔗 is not displayed, click ▸ on the Standard toolbar to display all the buttons.

■ The Insert Hyperlink dialog box appears.

**Can I make a graphic a
hyperlink?**

Yes. If your document contains
a graphic, such as an AutoShape
or clip art image, you can make
the graphic a hyperlink. To
make a graphic a hyperlink,
click the graphic and then
perform steps **2** to **7**, starting
on page 212.

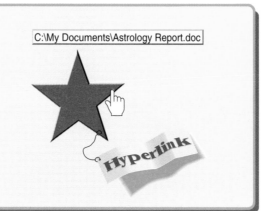

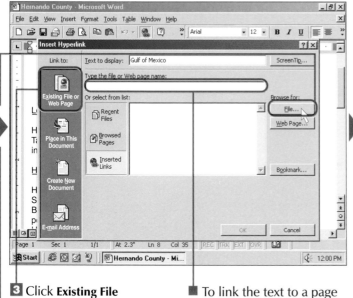

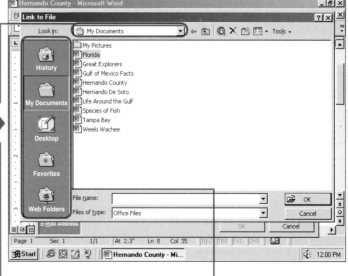

3 Click **Existing File
or Web Page**.

4 To link the text to
a document on your
computer or network,
click **File**.

■ To link the text to a page
on the Web, click this area
and then type the address
of the Web page (example:
www.maran.com). Then
skip to step **7** on page 214.

■ The Link to File dialog
box appears.

■ This area shows the
location of the displayed
documents. You can click
this area to change the
location.

■ This area allows you
to access commonly
used folders. To display
the contents of a folder,
click the folder.

*Note: For information on
the commonly used folders,
see the top of page 23.*

CONTINUED

You can easily identify hyperlinks in your document. Hyperlinks appear underlined and in color.

EARTH WISE ENTERPRISES
We care about the environment.

All products created and marketed by Earth Wise Enterprises are designed to increase awareness of environmental issues around the world.

A list of our main types of products is presented below. To find out more about the products in any category, select the category name.

Tree planting kits

Recycle bins

Compost kits

CREATE A HYPERLINK (CONTINUED)

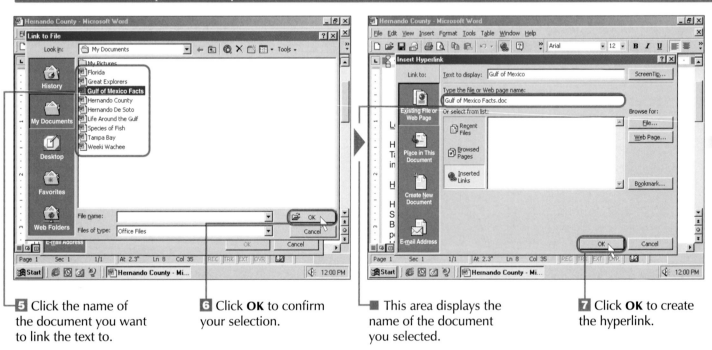

5 Click the name of the document you want to link the text to.

6 Click **OK** to confirm your selection.

■ This area displays the name of the document you selected.

7 Click **OK** to create the hyperlink.

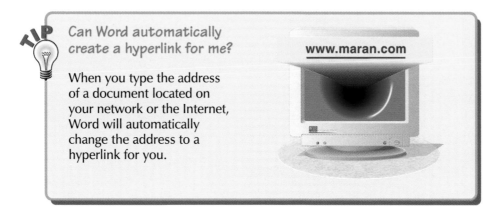

**Can Word automatically
create a hyperlink for me?**

When you type the address
of a document located on
your network or the Internet,
Word will automatically
change the address to a
hyperlink for you.

www.maran.com

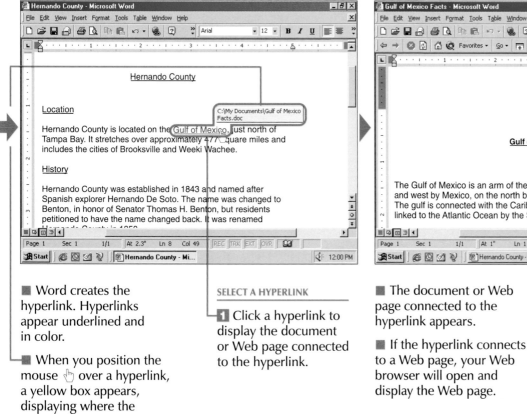

■ Word creates the
hyperlink. Hyperlinks
appear underlined and
in color.

■ When you position the
mouse 🖑 over a hyperlink,
a yellow box appears,
displaying where the
hyperlink will take you.

SELECT A HYPERLINK

1 Click a hyperlink to
display the document
or Web page connected
to the hyperlink.

■ The document or Web
page connected to the
hyperlink appears.

■ If the hyperlink connects
to a Web page, your Web
browser will open and
display the Web page.

2 When you finish
reviewing the document
or Web page, click ☒
to close the window.

SAVE A DOCUMENT AS A WEB PAGE

You can save a document as a Web page. This lets you place the document on the Internet or your company's intranet.

An intranet is a small version of the Internet within a company or organization.

SAVE A DOCUMENT AS A WEB PAGE

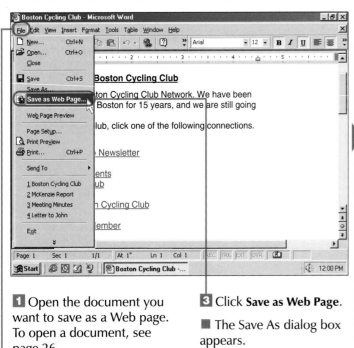

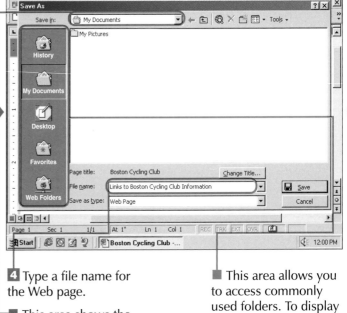

1 Open the document you want to save as a Web page. To open a document, see page 26.

2 Click **File**.

3 Click **Save as Web Page**.

■ The Save As dialog box appears.

4 Type a file name for the Web page.

■ This area shows the location where Word will store the Web page. You can click this area to change the location.

■ This area allows you to access commonly used folders. To display the contents of a folder, click the folder.

Note: For information on the commonly used folders, see the top of page 23.

TIP

How do I make my Web page available for other people to view?

After you save a document as a Web page, you can transfer the page to a computer that stores Web pages, called a Web server. Once you publish a Web page on a Web server, the page will be available for other people to view. For more information on publishing a Web page, contact your network administrator or Internet service provider.

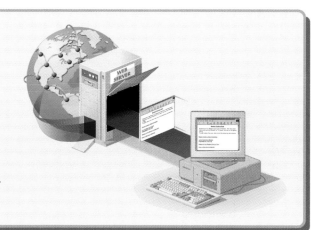

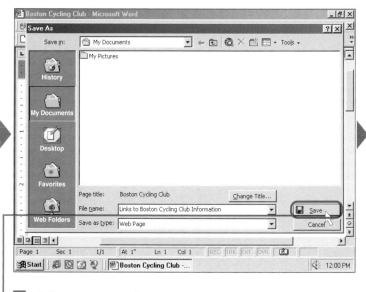

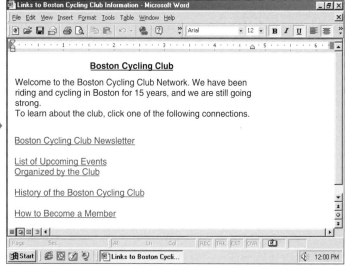

5 Click **Save** to save the document as a Web page.

■ Word saves the document as a Web page and displays the document in the Web Layout view. This view displays the document as it will appear on the Web.

Note: For more information on the views, see page 34.

INDEX

INDEX

INDEX

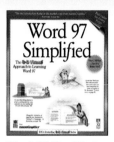

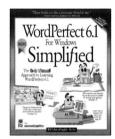

OVER 6 MILLION

OTHER **3-D Visual**
SERIES

TEACH YOURSELF VISUALLY SERIES

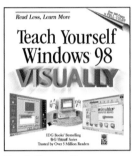
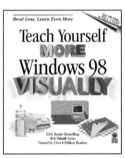
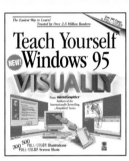

IDG BOOKS ®

TRADE & INDIVIDUAL ORDERS	EDUCATIONAL ORDERS & DISCOUNTS	CORPORATE ORDERS FOR 3-D VISUAL™ SERIES
Phone: **(800) 762-2974**	Phone: **(800) 434-2086**	Phone: **(800) 469-6616**
or **(317) 596-5200**	(8:30 a.m.–5:00 p.m., CST, weekdays)	(8 a.m.–5 p.m., EST, weekdays)
(8 a.m.–6 p.m., CST, weekdays)	FAX : **(317) 596-5499**	FAX : **(905) 890-9434**
FAX : **(800) 550-2747**		
or **(317) 596-5692**		

Qty	ISBN	Title	Price	Total

Shipping & Handling Charges

	Description	First book	Each add'l. book	Total
Domestic	Normal	$4.50	$1.50	$
	Two Day Air	$8.50	$2.50	$
	Overnight	$18.00	$3.00	$
International	Surface	$8.00	$8.00	$
	Airmail	$16.00	$16.00	$
	DHL Air	$17.00	$17.00	$

Subtotal _____

CA residents add
applicable sales tax _____

IN, MA and MD
residents add
5% sales tax _____

IL residents add
6.25% sales tax _____

RI residents add
7% sales tax _____

TX residents add
8.25% sales tax _____

Shipping _____

Total _____

Ship to:

Name _____

Address _____

Company _____

City/State/Zip _____

Daytime Phone _____

Payment: ☐ Check to IDG Books (US Funds Only)
 ☐ Visa ☐ Mastercard ☐ American Express

Card # _____ Exp. _____ Signature _____

maranGraphics™